WHAT'S FOOD GOT TO DO WITH IT?

LESSONS FROM FOOD LAB: TEACHING COOKING TO YOUNG ADULTS WITH LEARNING DISABILITIES

What's Food Got to Do With It?

Lessons from Food Lab: Teaching Cooking to Young Adults with Learning Disabilities

Carole Noveck

iUniverse, Inc.
Bloomington

What's Food Got to Do With It?
Lessons from Food Lab: Teaching Cooking to
Young Adults with Learning Disabilities

iUniverse books may be ordered through booksellers or by contacting:

iUniverse
1663 Liberty Drive
Bloomington, IN 47403
www.iuniverse.com
1-800-Authors (1-800-288-4677)

Because of the dynamic nature of the Internet, any web addresses or links contained in this book may
have changed since publication and may no longer be valid.

Any people depicted in stock imagery provided by Thinkstock are models,
and such images are being used for illustrative purposes only.

Certain stock imagery © Thinkstock.

ISBN: 978-1-4620-0055-5 (sc)
ISBN: 978-1-4502-9471-3 (ebk)

Printed in the United States of America

iUniverse rev. date: 3/31/2011

This book is dedicated with much appreciation to the Threshold students who shared their recipes, their good humor, and their enthusiasm for cooking.

Acknowledgments

This material could never have been put together without the cooperation of all of the Threshold faculty and families who contributed their recipes and their insights.

My deep gratitude and appreciation to my family—my husband Ray, my son Evan and especially to my daughter Loren, for their guidance, support, and professional advice.

Many thanks to Adeline Burlington for being my wonderful first reader, and to Leslie Corris for the walks and talks.

CONTENTS

1. A MESSAGE FROM THE AUTHOR.....................1

2. INTRODUCTION TO THE THRESHOLD PROGRAM AT LESLEY UNIVERSITY 7

3. WHAT IS FOOD LAB?............................10

4. BRIDGE YEAR 21

5. MOTIVATION 31

6. CONNECTION TO HERITAGE AND TRADITIONS 51

7. ISLANDS OF COMPETENCE........................68

8. RESPECT FOR DIFFERENCES.......................81

9. LEARNED HELPLESSNESS........................103

10. PERSONALITY FACTORS AND PERFORMANCE IN THE KITCHEN 121

11. CHILDHOOD OBESITY...........................138

12. CONCLUSION..................................142

REFERENCES: 144

RECIPE INDEX 146

CHAPTER 1

A MESSAGE FROM THE AUTHOR

Hello.

What *does* food have to do with it? Although I began my career teaching young adults with learning disabilities about the world of work, I realized, after working with this population for almost twenty years, that I needed to learn more about them. It was only when I began to teach independent living skills in a Food Lab class that I began to get the full picture of who they were, how they learned, and what influenced their lives.

The author of a cookbook that I read as I was doing some research for that class mentioned something that intrigued me. Molly Wizenberg (2009) said, "When I walk into my kitchen today, I am not alone. Whether we know it or not, none of us is. We bring fathers and mothers and kitchen tables, and every meal we have ever eaten. Food is never just food. It's also a way of getting at something else: who we are, who we have been, and who we want to be." Each week, as I work with the students, I become increasingly aware of all the other bodies, histories, personalities, and life and learning styles that are in the lab with us.

I know I am fortunate to be one of those few people to combine my career and my much-enjoyed avocation. It all started when asked in fourth or fifth grade what I wanted to be when I grew up: I responded "psychiatrist." I don't remember exactly what gave me that idea or even introduced that term into my childish vocabulary. Then in middle school (it was called junior high in those archaic days) when we were given an option to do some community service, I chose to work with children with what was then called "mental retardation" in an inner-city school. I really enjoyed the relationships I developed with the children and recognized that I particularly liked to see the growth that they exhibited. Although their development might have been delayed and the progress was slow, there was a definite, visible change over the year in their ability to complete some very basic tasks. From there, I went on to major in psychology in college and complete my thesis on motivation in children, using special-education students as my subjects. Much to my parents' dismay, I did not want to teach, although I recognized the value in the security and the benefits of that career. I think I knew I preferred developing a more one-on-one relationship with my clients/students. I took a summer internship with the State of New Jersey Vocational Rehabilitation Commission as a counselor and upon graduation turned that experience into my initial career. My area of special interest was students with learning challenges. At that time, learning disabilities were just being recognized as a disorder that would require long-term assistance, training, and funding to achieve appropriate employment goals. From that point, I was hooked on working with young people with disabilities, helping them discover and develop vocational skills. So, the vocational component of my future was easy to foresee. The avocational piece was a little more difficult to predict.

I did not grow up in a family that valued cooking or food preparation. My mother's primary interest was watching her daughter's and her own food consumption so we would be able to control our weight. She had a limited selection of menus, and an even more restricted choice of acceptable spices. Onions and garlic were not allowed to enter the house and were not even permissible in a restaurant meal. Salt wasn't viewed very kindly because of its water retention properties; even pepper was suspicious because it might taste too good. However, sugar and cinnamon were valued because my mom loved to bake. She was famous for some of her creations and took pride and satisfaction in baking the best cookies, pies, and cakes. She somehow decided that if we controlled our intake of good, healthy, solid food, we could reserve our calories for dessert. Information about carbohydrates, proteins, and food pyramids was not in style back then so I was not very aware of good nutrition. Bread, pasta, potatoes, and rice were not part of my regular diet and were foods reserved for special occasions. I always wondered, as I ate my daily lunch of dry tuna fish in a baby food jar with a few carrot sticks, why and how everyone else was able to eat those delicious-looking juicy sandwiches.

Therefore, I was very surprised when I went to a high school reunion, many years later, to discover that one of the primary memories of one of my friends, with whom I spent many hours studying, dancing, talking, and laughing was the cookies that my mother made with us. Judy recalled in detail how we made the dough for peppermint twists, how we colored the dough, shaped the cookie canes, baked them, and enjoyed sharing the sweet and crispy cookies as they emerged from the oven. Judy didn't recall the names of the songs we listened to; the homework assignments we shared, even the names of our crushes, but she had vivid, fond memories of the baked goods we shared.

I still wasn't aware of my relative food/taste deprivation until I met my husband-to-be's family. He grew up in a traditional Jewish home, where chicken fat, challah, and spices were part of every week's meals. The good smells and flavors of Eastern European cooking were part of his history. And then, his father was assigned to a job in France. When my mother-in-law returned to the USA after spending five years living in Europe, among her most vivid reminders of their time abroad was the food she remembered eating and learning to prepare. Although she had been raised observing kosher food practice, when she thought about her experiences living in a different culture, the food memories were among the most significant to her. Changing her diet because it was too challenging to comply with some of the restrictions with which she had been brought up was a cultural adjustment. She learned about cooking with butter, eating sauces and meats that she had never tasted, seeing and smelling foods that she had only read about. It was a whole body experience. She never reverted back to her old routine when she returned to the U.S. She brought her broadened palette and new recipes back with her and made them her new standard.

When my husband and I got married and began to live independently and I started cooking on my own, I knew I wanted to follow his tradition of tasty, spicy, interesting foods rather than being confined by my own limited food memories. Dessert always continued to be important to me, but I began to enjoy making meals that were more complex.

Because I had a full-time job and a long commute in the beginning of my marriage, I didn't have tons of time to cook complicated meals. But I always wanted to research and try things that could be relatively healthy, not too expensive, and not too time consuming, without sacrificing flavor.

And then, we were lucky enough for my husband to be offered his own job rotation in Europe. Taking our two little children to Switzerland gave me the same eye-opening experience that my mother-in-law had many years before. Even without language fluency, and with limited cooking supplies, by absorption and observation, I began to broaden my cooking taste and confidence. Being exposed to new cooking techniques and equipment also opened my eyes. I began to use a precious Cuisinart food processor before many people in the USA were even aware of this amazing contraption. Upon our return home, I was offered opportunity to demonstrate this new invention in department stores and cooking schools. I decided to try to develop a second career. However, because I never wanted to let go of my original interest in working with people, I concurrently enrolled in graduate school part-time for a master's degree in counseling. I began a crazy time in my life. I was teaching cooking classes, demonstrating techniques, taking classes, studying, and fitting in some time with my family. When I completed my degree, the job market was tight for careers in social service. While I searched for a job in my field, I progressed from teaching cooking to catering to designing kitchens. And then, my whole life recycled. Coincidentally while working with a client drawing plans for a new kitchen, I met a woman with whom I had worked in my very first job. She told me about a job opening for a vocational counselor in an agency for young adults with special needs. Here I was back in my old groove, working in the vocational department of a residential placement facility for young adults with learning disabilities.

Reality hit once again several years later, when my husband was reassigned, this time to Massachusetts. I was fortunate enough to be able to once again recycle my skills and experience when I found a position in the vocational department at the Threshold Program at Lesley University. I have enjoyed many years working in that position. Teaching and advising young adults with learning challenges, I observed the growth and development of the students as I helped them find the best match for jobs in the community.

And then, suddenly, six years ago inspiration hit. I had the craving and the fortune to try to put all my skills and interests together. I asked to teach the Food Lab course, and that's when I slowly became aware of something fascinating and remarkable. Using my fondness for cooking, and my interest and experience with working with young adults with learning differences, I realized I learned so much about each of the students as we cooked together. I could see their family histories and dynamics, their learning styles, and their personalities, displayed in this class. I became aware that I was witnessing their backgrounds and histories as we cooked together. Although I thought I had been familiar with the students and their families when we worked together to find and keep jobs, there was another level of engagement that I had never before recognized. I knew I needed to learn more about this phenomenon.

I feel so fortunate to be able to combine my creative outlet, my responsibility to feed my family nutritious, tasty, reasonably simple meals, and my career, helping young adults as they begin their independent lives.

In this publication, I will discuss some of the concepts that have led to my new comprehension and deep appreciation of the huge impact food, food preparation, and consumption can have on each of us. I want to inform other educators of the possibilities for mutual learning that can develop through the process, so they consider this learning opportunity with their students.

I have combined my insights and ideas with some of the wonderful recipes that the Threshold students have chosen and prepared to illustrate some of the issues I have addressed. I am sharing all this with you -students, families, and educators- so you can join me in this culinary learning adventure.

Bon appétit,
Carole

RECIPES FROM FOOD LAB

The recipes that are integrated into the text of this book are all selections that the Threshold Program students chose, planned, and produced in their Food Lab classes over the past few years. Preparing these recipes with the class offered me insights that changed my understanding of the ways in which students learn and interact. Helping them trace their roots, expand their learning options, develop respect for one another, recognize their areas of competence, and/or fight the learned helplessness that might have set limits on their growth taught me a great deal. I gained awareness of the possibility that lessons in food preparation may provide a much broader range of knowledge than merely teaching someone how to cook a meal to ease hunger. These classes broaden knowledge, and teach respect and appreciation of other people. Each recipe gave me some new understanding of the student, their family background and/or their learning process. The recipes illustrate the potential of using food preparation as a learning tool for educators and families.

CHAPTER 2

INTRODUCTION TO THE THRESHOLD PROGRAM AT LESLEY UNIVERSITY

To celebrate the hundredth year of Lesley University, in Cambridge, Massachusetts, a centennial publication was produced in 2010. Several individuals with a relationship with The Threshold Program, including Arlyn Roffman, PhD, the founder and former director of the program, the author, and another colleague realized that it was important to include the history of Threshold in this educational piece. The material below is based on the research we completed for this project.

In the early 1980s, the idea of transition from high school to post-high school programming for students with special needs was just beginning. Chapter 766, the Massachusetts law guaranteeing a free and appropriate public education (FAPE) for students with special needs, had been passed just a few years before in 1974, followed even more recently by its federal equivalent, Public Law 94-142, The Education for All Handicapped Children Act. Despite the great step forward in special education represented by these pieces of legislation, their impact was initially limited largely to elementary and middle schools or to programs for children with varying levels of retardation (Grossman, 1983). The ongoing needs of older youth with disabilities went unaddressed for several more years until educators and policy makers finally began to recognize that many disabling conditions persist into adolescence and are never outgrown. Only then did they acknowledge the associated lifelong challenges and mandate that long-term goals extending beyond the high school years be addressed in the Individualized Education Programs (IEPs) of secondary school special-education students with both severe and moderate disabilities (Sitlington and Frank, 1990).

A major turning point occurred in 1984, when Madeline Wills, assistant secretary for the US Office of Special Education and Rehabilitative Services (OSERS), wrote a paper (Wills, 1984) that propelled the transition movement into federal policy. Although Wills, like her predecessors, described transition in narrow, job-related terms, she did recognize the need for a broader range when she added that "success in social, personal, leisure, and other adult roles enhances opportunities both to obtain employment and enjoy its benefits" (p.1, emphasis added). Halpern (1985) also noted the significance of training and experience with independent living skills when he wrote that "living successfully in one's community should be the primary target of transitional services" (p.480), a perspective that opened the door to a more holistic approach toward transition that validated the thinking behind the Threshold model, then several years old.

In 1981, when there were few options after high school for young adults with disabilities, Lesley College, as it was called at that time, took a risk and supported the development of Threshold, the innovative transition program that Dr. Roffman proposed. Now, 28 years later, the Threshold Program continues to proudly prepare students with significant special needs for work, community integration, and lifelong learning.

The proposal indicated that the independent living component of the program would prepare students for community life. A series of courses would focus on such practicalities as money management (banking and budgeting), apartment living skills (meal planning and preparation, cleaning), sexuality, and daily living skills, such as personal hygiene and basic medical self-care.

From those parameters, Food Lab began. This required weekly course for second-year students was designed to offer a basic introduction to cooking and serving foods that the students would be able to prepare when they graduated and moved into their own apartments. As years went by and instructors changed, although the model and the goals remained, it became obvious that many life skills, in addition to the most elementary, could be taught within the parameters of the Food Lab syllabus.

This class was an opportunity for the students to gain remedial education in both math and reading skills. They learned more social skills and gained an appreciation for their similarities and differences based on their heritage, upbringing, and personal taste. Students were also introduced to the rewards of serving others, while increasing their pride and self-respect through performing community service learning projects such as helping cook and serve meals in food pantries and conducting bake sales. This learning model combined the utilization of their emerging skills with the planning and administration of the self-selected project (Roffman, Osten, Noveck, 2009).

A recent follow-up study described how successful Threshold has been in giving graduates the tools to continue their growth living independently and integrating into contemporary society (*see* Osten, 2009).

In the spring, a semi-formal dance is held at a local hotel honoring the current students and a broad array of alumni. For many of the students, this event represents a reminder of years in the past when they might not have had the friends or the confidence to attend and enjoy the social events sponsored by their high schools. Each year, on that night, friends, administrators, and teachers, who know and value every student, surround them. It is a cheery, glorious celebration. It is also a time for the faculty and administration to gaze with wonder at the success that so many of the graduates have achieved. They come to the dance, all dressed up, with their spouses or their new engagement rings, sharing tales of their jobs and developing families. It is a remarkable view of the success of the Threshold Program.

At the graduation celebration at the conclusion of Transition Year, another of the third-year options, we asked the graduates to describe the sources of satisfaction and pride they had developed over the year. Almost every student mentioned their ability to cook and to use the cookbook they had helped put together as one of the areas they most valued. Hearing this information intensified my awareness of the merit of Food Lab and the confidence building that this class provided.

In the following chapters, I will try to identify the broad concepts I have recognized. Because the recipes that the students have selected and prepared have been the means to develop these insights, the recipes are indexed to the specific topic that contributed to my learning.

CHAPTER 3

WHAT IS FOOD LAB?

I believe that in this complex world in which young people are growing up and trying to find their own place, any means by which educators and families can learn more about their students and help them navigate through the confusion is helpful. Basic home economics disappeared from the core curricula in most school districts in the late 1970s. Some learning tools might have been lost in the transition. I believe that if home economics could be reintroduced into the core curriculum in late elementary or middle school, society might take a new look at a process to discover the essence of the individuals in the classroom and their backgrounds. Another way to identify learning styles may be considered. An alternative route to helping students develop competence and confidence and a different way to develop respect for differences might surface. Please join me as I describe what I have learned in Food Lab that might intrigue other educators.

In 1943, psychologist Abraham Maslow, in his paper *A Theory of Human Motivation*, defined a hierarchy of needs that described many realities of personal experience. He felt that human beings want to strive for higher levels of consciousness and fulfillment, but must first satisfy the most basic needs before they can move to the next level. The very first needs are the biological, physiological needs for oxygen, food, and water. I began to think that maybe everyone, whether it was a well-educated, sophisticated older adult, a teenager, or a student in a program for young adults with special needs, shared this requirement to consider and resolve their most basic needs before they could move on to recognize and attempt to fulfill the next level of needs and desires. I questioned whether the preparation and consumption of food revealed more about people than just what entered their digestive tracts. As I reflected on my work with young adults with learning challenges, I became aware that in teaching the Food Lab class I was learning more about the students, their learning styles, their family backgrounds and traditions than I did in all the other courses I taught.

I began to think about my own experiences as the mother of a son with some learning issues. I understood the complications and frustrations of dealing with the issues and systems, politically and academically, that made it so challenging to resolve some of the situations that confronted our children. Sometimes, it was so difficult to control my desire to just do something for my son, Evan, rather than have him struggle to comply. I knew that I had to let him take his own path to resolve the challenges, but it concerned and hurt me that he would not achieve what he wanted and needed to do to move forward. I was empathetic with the parents who wanted so badly to smooth the bumps for their children, and who thought that they were doing their best by not giving their children the opportunities to fail. I am totally respectful of their sincere desire to do everything they could to prepare their children for the future. From my hard-earned perspective having an adult child with attention deficit disorder, I have learned some strategies that sometimes worked to assist a young adult to try new things. I hoped that I would be able to use, in Food Lab, some of what I had learned with my own son, as well as with the many other students who have participated in this class. I also hoped I would be able to encourage both the students and their families to take some leaps. I would try to provide a safety net whenever possible and would offer flexibility and encouragement to remind everyone, myself included, that we didn't need perfection in cooking and that there wasn't only one right way, but were many alternative routes to preparing a meal. It seemed possible that I might be able to help the students and their families learn some basic recipes and cooking techniques that could prepare them for their future, and might also provide the foundation to continue their own history with food. I hoped students would also be able to start to satisfy their most basic need and begin the journey to reach the other levels.

Rachel Narins said, in Michael Pollan's Favorite Food Quotes: "I always say, 'don't yuck someone's yum.' Not a diet strategy but an important food lesson. There is someone out there who likes deep-fried sheep eyeballs, and, well, more power to them." This quote provided a basic philosophy to Food Lab. The class met every week for two hours in a simple kitchen in one of the dormitories. The kitchen had a refrigerator/freezer, a cook top, double ovens, cabinets with work surfaces, a small pantry, and a table. This was far from a fancy model kitchen but serviceable and comfortable for a small group. There were usually between four and seven students in each class, which met in four different sections to offer every second-year student the chance to have this learning opportunity. In the first session of the year, the students were informed of the expectations of the class. I told them that we were going to learn, through practical experience, how to find, analyze, and prepare recipes that would be pretty simple to make, requiring no more than one hour total preparation time at a cost of no more than $20 to serve four people. We discussed how to figure out approximate costs of recipes using general food prices. Basic nutrition was an important guideline for every main course recipe, and we tried to figure out ways to make even sweet dessert recipes less caloric or fat laden. We discussed the food pyramid and talked about the wide array of foods that could offer proteins and dairy options to develop well-balanced meals. A food survey was one of their first assignments. I needed to know if anyone had food allergies or any other eating prohibitions. I also wanted to know both their most and least favorite foods. I asked which ethnic cuisines they enjoyed.

The idea of having respect for one another's food choices was a basic premise. I told them stories of other classes where members of the class had drastically broadened their culinary repertoire by just trying one bite of a new food. Although students were never told that they had to eat anything where they had some legitimate concern, whether it is a health, religious, or cultural prohibition, I tried to find systems to allow each student to expand their eating experiences. If there were any defined food allergies where there could be some negative consequences or a chance of someone developing a severe reaction, we tried to eliminate that element from every recipe. Certain nuts, particularly peanuts, and spices that had potential to cause problems were replaced every time they appeared in the recipe. When there was some other prohibition, as in a kosher tradition or another set of standards, we studied how an ingredient could be removed and substituted with some other ingredient that would not impact on the taste or texture of the recipe, but could allow people to eat new foods. When one student, for example, shared a gluten allergy, we had to reconfigure recipes and be constantly alert to find alternative foods that could deliver flavor and nutrition while avoiding the particular items that triggered the negative reaction.

As Malcolm Gladwell said: "Practice isn't the thing you do once you're good. It's the thing you do that makes you good." As I planned this class, I had several goals besides learning basic nutrition and cooking techniques. I hoped that I could help students develop more confidence as well as competence, not just in their cooking, but in the way they made decisions and lived on their own. I hoped that with practice in reading recipes, planning a shopping list, preparing the food, setting the table, and enjoying their meals, they would "get good" at living in their own space.

My plan offered some responsibility and leadership experience to the person who submitted the recipe for that week and served as head chef. The students were told that everyone would have a task each week. The head chef introduced the recipe and assigned jobs to each of the team members. The sous chef provided primary support for the head chef in the cooking process. Some recipes were more complicated and required every participant to take charge of one step. Other recipes did not have as many steps but did offer opportunities to try new techniques or new equipment. Mashing potatoes with a potato ricer was a great adventure; scraping a lemon for lemon rind with a micro plane offered new learning options. Most weeks we found at least one less familiar term, appliance, or ingredient to explore. Preheating ovens, using timers, and rinsing dishes before they went into the dishwasher were very basic but important lessons. The students who were neither the head chef nor the sous chef chose some other important tasks in addition to the direct cooking jobs. Unloading the dishwasher at the beginning of class offered some thoughtful activity. Counting the number of participants in the class that day, figuring out which plates and cutlery would match the particular meal we were preparing, and reserving those that were going to go directly to the serving table, and which could be stored for another meal, took some learning in the first few weeks. Setting the table, folding napkins, and using trivets when hot food was served were other thoughtful steps. Learning to clean up as they cooked, rather than dumping the cooking utensils in the sink and coming back after the meal to face the mess, took a bit of time to develop. However, once that practice was established, almost every student recognized the value of that procedure. One mother, after winter break, mentioned how much she appreciated her daughter's new comfort level in the kitchen and the clean-up habits she had acquired. A student with vision issues taught her teammates to sanitize the counters using a grid method. The sections of the counter were divided into segments and each piece was cleaned in an orderly manner.

Using cloth towels rather than paper towels was an issue to talk about. I provided many towels, which I washed and bleached each week, because I wanted the students to get in the habit of using cloth instead of grabbing another two or three paper towels and then tossing them. It seemed worthwhile to me to save a few trees without sacrificing any sanitation. It took a while for that new practice to be institutionalized for some class members, but most caught on relatively quickly.

I always wore an apron during this class and offered aprons to any student who wanted to borrow one for the class. Initially only those students with some prior culinary training were comfortable putting on aprons. As the class developed, more students recognized the value of having their clothes covered and the availability of a garment that let them wipe their hands or use the cloth to grab something hot in a convenient way. After we were given a few professional chefs' jackets, I offered a jacket to the head chef each week. There was some reluctance when we first received the gift, but after a while students vied for the opportunity to don the jacket. Several students even dreamed about earning the "toque," the white chef's hat. One piece of headgear that I required was either a barrette or a rubber band to tie back long hair (male or female) after witnessing a long ponytail be ignited by a random flare-up near the stove. After that frightening experience, it was easy to enforce that rule.

Kitchen safety was another element introduced. Personal protection, using hot pads and trivets, maintaining control over the height of the flame or the temperature of the oven, standing back from a sizzling pot, inserting food into boiling liquid slowly were issues that were discovered as the recipes called for those techniques. Experiential learning, well recognized as a common method for teaching skills to people with learning challenges, was the prime technique used in this class. There could never be a better learning laboratory than a cooking class. John Dewey, a well-recognized educational theorist, believed in experiential learning, as did Seneca, way back when. The value of having students take leadership in the classroom was also recognized in the historic texts. Learning to open a cooking container after steaming in the microwave was something that could not be taught by just describing the intense heat that could be emitted from the pot. Practicing using a hot pad, and opening the cooking chamber away from the body, had to develop by feeling the steam burn the eyes, and the skin by just being close to the heat. It took only one time and one slightly frizzled student before everyone recognized the respect that the microwave requires.

Having patience was one more skill that needed practice. Removing soft cookies off the baking sheet immediately after taking the cookies from the oven and watching them fold up was disappointing. French toast or pancakes didn't work as well until the batter had the chance to bubble or firm up before each piece was flipped. Checking each piece of meat to see if it was cooked thoroughly also took some patience. Although it was tempting, taking a bite of a chocolate kiss cookie as soon as it came out of the oven provided a painful lesson in patience. One singed tongue said it all. When preparing a multi-course meal, reading and analyzing the recipes to decide which course had to start first, and when to start cooking the next piece, took some time and consideration.

Almost every year someone asked to prepare some variety of "Kiss" cookies. They had usually prepared the cookies with some favorite family member and the recipe was delivered with feelings of warmth and acceptance. Both the plain and the peanut butter variety were very popular. The only challenge was waiting until the cookie was thoroughly cooled until it was tasted. The chocolate kiss retained a great deal of heat and it was not fun to see someone's mouth burn if they were too tempted to taste it before it had cooled down sufficiently.

CHOCOLATE KISS COOKIES
Makes 36 cookies

INGREDIENTS
1 cup butter, softened
½ cup sugar
1 tsp vanilla extract
1 egg, beaten well
1¾ cups flour
1 cup walnuts, finely chopped (optional)
1 package milk chocolate kisses
Confectioner's sugar (optional)
NOTE: If you are not using walnuts, you must increase amount of flour to 2 ½ cups

DIRECTIONS
If using electric mixer, cream butter, adding sugar and vanilla gradually. Beat egg by mixing well with fork or whisk. Add to butter mixture. If you are not using mixer, combine butter and sugar well, then add egg and vanilla.

Gradually add in flour (and nuts if using) and combine well.

Cover dough and chill in refrigerator for at least 1 hour.

Preheat oven to 350 degrees.

Remove dough from refrigerator. Unwrap foil from chocolate kisses and wrap each piece of chocolate with ball of dough. Cover kiss completely.

Place on ungreased cookie sheet—leave 2 inches of space between each cookie.

Bake for 10 minutes, until center of cookie looks set and edges are brown.

May roll in confectioner's sugar while warm.

Cool completely on wire racks before tasting.

Store in airtight containers.

If you have never made pancakes from scratch you are in for a wonderful surprise. It is quite simple and the pancakes are light and fluffy. Each year, one of the more reluctant cooks asked shyly if we could make pancakes. They were usually surprised when we took out the basic ingredients instead of the box of pancake mix. And they were always pleased to see how much they and their classmates enjoyed the finished product. Chocolate chips are a wonderful addition, but blueberries or other fruit, or even just plain pancakes, work well also. The only "but" is the need to have patience to wait until the pancakes bubble and firm up before flipping them or removing them from the skillet.

CHOCOLATE CHIP PANCAKES
Serves 4 (12 pancakes)

INGREDIENTS:
1 cup flour
2 tsps baking powder
2 tbs sugar
½ tsp salt
1 egg
½ to ¾ cup milk (add water to thin batter)
2 tbs butter, melted then cooled
½ cup chocolate chips
Syrup or powdered sugar to serve

DIRECTIONS:
Stir or whisk flour, baking powder, sugar, and salt together.
Beat egg, milk, and butter until well blended.
Pour milk mixture over dry ingredients and stir until just moistened. Don't beat too much or the batter will become tough.
Stir in chocolate chips.
Grease griddle or skillet with margarine or spray with cooking spray. Heat until water beads when sprinkled on pan.
Pour ½ cup batter on griddle and cook each pancake until holes begin to appear on top surface; turn each pancake over with spatula and cook other side. Cooking pancakes takes patience—don't rush. The pancakes will fall apart and lose texture if they are not well cooked.

Reserve cooked pancakes in oven preheated to 200 degrees to keep warm as you cook additional pancakes.

The reinforcement of learning in other classes was an additional goal for this class. Another required class for second-year students was Apartment Living, where the students were introduced to the realities of living independently. One of their assignments was to report on another country. Included in this project was the examination of the foods consumed there. By researching and preparing some of the meals that were consumed in the countries they explored, they expanded their knowledge of the country. So many things were revealed in the foods eaten in different countries. Local weather and growing conditions could be compared. The relative economy and the basic life styles could be inferred from some of the recipes. I encouraged students to cook something in Food Lab that they had discovered in their research and bring it to their other class when they presented their project. This opportunity broadened their learning, giving them an opportunity to use many senses besides the traditional reading and writing skills that are usually involved in a term project. We prepared and sampled many interesting dishes like *lomo saltado* from Peru, scones from England, and paella from Spain. This project strengthened the learning in both classes and taught us all some areas of similarities and differences among cultures and people. Several times, the students recognized certain flavors that crossed cultures. We were able to discuss how and why that occurred. Using taste and smell, they could learn the geographic transitions between nationalities in a way that book learning alone could not offer.

Adding food to a school project certainly expanded the learning process. For one assignment in Apartment Living class, students had to research the foods eaten in the region that they had investigated. There was so much to learn by preparing and tasting a recipe typical of that culture. Although paella can be complex, this version that Brandon selected offered learning and taste opportunities without all the time and complications.

PAELLA EXPRESS
Serves 4-6

INGREDIENTS
1/3 cup olive oil
1 small onion, peeled and minced
2-3 cloves of garlic, peeled and crushed
3-5 tbs fresh parsley, minced
1 generous pinch of saffron
1 tsp sugar
2 tbs (or 2 cubes) of chicken bouillon
1 8-oz can tomato sauce
3 boneless, skinless chicken breasts cut into large chunks
2 green peppers, seeded and sliced
1 red pepper, seeded and sliced
4 cups rice
7 cups water
NOTE: Traditional paella usually includes seafood. ¾-1 lb of raw peeled shrimp and/or scallops can be added for taste and texture.

DIRECTIONS
In large stockpot, warm olive oil and sauté onion, garlic, and parsley until onion is soft and clear. Add saffron, sugar, bouillon, tomato sauce, chicken chunks, and peppers and sauté together until chicken is white and thoroughly cooked.

Add rice and water and bring to boil. Add salt to taste. Cook for 5 minutes, stirring occasionally. (If using seafood, shrimp or scallops can be added now.)

Simmer covered for at least 10 more minutes, stirring occasionally. Check mixture. Add bit of water if rice is dry after 10 minutes. If mixture is too moist, remove cover and continue cooking for a few more minutes until it reaches desired texture.

CHAPTER 4

BRIDGE YEAR

The Threshold Program was initially designed as a two-year post-secondary program for young adults with learning disabilities who had the motivation to further develop their vocational and independent living skills. The director and faculty recognized after the first few years that, as with many recent high school graduates enrolled in traditional community-college programs, two years was not sufficient time for most students to develop the competence and confidence to put their recently developed skills to best use. An optional third-year program, Transition Year, was developed. In this ten-month program, the graduates moved into apartments in neighboring communities and received support finding jobs and living on their own. Again, it didn't take too long before it became apparent that there were also a few students each year who were just not ready to take the leap into living totally independently after only two years. Because of a delay in the development of either their vocational or independent living skills, they still needed a bit more time and training. The Bridge Year was developed. Each year, a small group of students remained on campus, exploring vocational options, working additional hours in their field placements, and getting more intense and individualized independent living skill training. We used Food Lab as a training field for an even wider array of skills. We had the time to go to the supermarket together and explore comparison shopping. We learned to set budgets and planned how we could maximize nutrition and taste with a limited budget. Incorporating the concept of Service Learning into the curriculum was a natural development.

Service Learning is a nationally recognized learning model where the students assume more leadership for their learning. The class chooses a theme for their studies and uses this theme as the focus of all their coursework. Service to a community was an essential element. It was inherent in the model that the service provider, the students, and the service recipient, an agency or program in the community, receive benefit from the program. Students take more responsibility for their learning by researching options and choosing, as a team, how they will accomplish their goals. Bridge Year felt like a perfect fit to test this concept.

In 2004-2005, all the forces came together to turn the year into a demonstration model for the concept of Service Learning. One of the participants, Tal, worked with a program for homeless children. She quickly recognized the challenges for a child living without a stable home. Tal described the complexities of surviving in a shelter. She told us how few possessions both the children and the center had available to them. She learned that the budget for the childcare center did not offer them the resources to teach the children like others who came from a different environment. Tal's passion led to a speedy selection of the theme and the recipient of our service project. A vote among the students resolved our decision to devote our efforts to learn about homelessness and plan a project that would develop funds to make a donation to the program. Considering all options, as a team the students decided that holding a bake sale could allow them to earn enough money to provide a reasonable contribution. I redesigned the Food Lab curriculum to give the students the opportunity to focus on ways to learn about those less fortunate than themselves. While we occasionally cooked other selections throughout that year, we concentrated on cooking food that could provide meals for citizens with greater needs. We prepared lasagna and salad for a shelter for victims of domestic violence; we cooked and served in a soup kitchen; and we participated in an Oxfam program that demonstrated how it felt to experience real long-term hunger. We began to bake and freeze brownies and other cookies or snack items that we could sell in our well-advertised bake sale, planned for a campus wide service day. We studied the path to homelessness through films, guest speakers, and field trips. We became involved with agencies in the community serving the population and provided volunteer service by stuffing envelopes for a health care agency for the homeless. Visiting one of the long-term stay facilities that the health care program provided and eating lunch with the program participants was an eye-opening experience. Chatting with drug addicts in recovery, with ex-convicts who had become homeless, and with young single mothers offered the best lessons. The students had a much better picture of the realities that we were talking about as we discussed addiction and mental illness. Our bake sale was a great success both financially and personally. Each student assumed leadership for one facet of the planning and execution of the sale. They selected their responsibilities based on their growing competence and confidence in one area. Brian managed organization and site planning; Matt handled finances and sales; Cubby helped with physical set-up and communication; Tal took leadership in baking and wrapping the products. When the students delivered the final donation to the service recipient with great pride, they recognized the value of what they had learned while simultaneously earning a sizeable donation for the charity of their choice.

Another year, one of the participants expressed his sincere concern for the wildlife and environment. We invited a faculty member in the Natural Science Department of Lesley University to cooperate with us. Dr. Morimoto adopted the Bridge Year program that year. He took us on bird walks and taught us how to recognize the array of natural sounds in our neighborhood. He gave suggestions for field trips that we could take and even consulted and offered suggestions on the agencies where our donation could be put to best use. Visiting a natural history museum and a farm, watching films about animals and wildlife, and reading about global warming and ecology all contributed to our learning. It also was an opportunity for cross-college integration. The Bridge Year students were natural ambassadors to welcome an esteemed professor in the regular college who otherwise might never have had the opportunity to really get to know the Threshold population. Our bake sale that year was part of the Lesley University Earth Day celebration and was a huge success for both the students and the National Wildlife Association.

Bryan came to Cambridge all the way from the state of Washington. He was far from home and had been brought up by an adoring mother who gave much of herself to Bryan. She told him that he could do and have everything. It just took while for Bryan to have the same faith in himself that his mother did... During Bridge Year, he began to develop his strengths and confidence. Watching him bloom that year and use his interests and abilities was a graphic example of what another year to learn and grow can do for some young adults. His role as the "business manager" of our Service learning project gave him pride and satisfaction. The taste of his scrumptious pizza pleased everyone.

DEEP DISH PIZZA
Makes one 14-inch deep dish pizza

INGREDIENTS
Dough
1 envelope Rapid Rise yeast
1 tbs sugar
1 tsp salt
1 cup warm water (120-130 degree)—baby bathwater temperature
2½ to 3 cups all-purpose flour
3 tbs vegetable oil
2 tsp cornmeal
(NOTE: Store bought pizza dough works fine. This is a challenge if you have never yet prepared yeast dough from scratch.)

Topping
1 lb lean ground beef or ground turkey (optional: use only if you want meatballs on top of pizza)
3 cups shredded mozzarella cheese
2 14-oz cans diced tomatoes, well drained
1 tsp oregano leaves
½ cup shredded parmesan cheese
½ cup shredded cheddar cheese

DIRECTIONS:

If making dough from scratch: In large bowl, combine undissolved yeast, sugar, and salt. Stir in water. If yeast is alive, bubbles should begin to develop immediately. Add one cup of flour and vegetable oil. Stir and gradually add flour to make soft dough. Let the dough tell you when you have added enough flour. Put dough onto floured surface and knead until smooth and elastic, about 8-10 minutes. Cover dough with cloth and let rest for 10 minutes.

Preheat oven to 500 degrees. Roll dough out into 16-inch circle to fit lightly greased 14-inch deep dish pizza pan that has been sprinkled with corn meal. Press dough into bottom of pan and up sides to 1½ inch border. If using premade dough, roll out and place onto pizza pan in same way.

Sprinkle dough with mozzarella cheese. Add tomatoes, oregano, and parmesan cheese.

If using meat, form tiny meatballs and sauté quickly in skillet. Meat should not be cooked through because it will continue to cook when baking.

Place meatballs, if using, on top. Sprinkle with cheddar cheese.

Place in preheated oven and immediately reduce temperature to 400 degrees.

Bake 20-25 minutes until crust is golden brown.

Remove from oven and cool on rack for 10 minutes before serving.

Rice Krispie treats must be a part of eating history for most Americans. We all remember the sweet, crunchy, sticky flavor and texture. It was surprising that no matter how many packets of the treats we prepared for the bake sale, we always sold out immediately, with people wanting to place orders for additional pieces. We began to make many extras of several different varieties, and they were all gone by the end of the sale. For the Bridge Year students, this product contributed to the whole learning experience.

OLD FAVORITE RICE KRISPIE TREATS
24 bars

INGREDIENTS
¼ cup unsalted butter (1/2 stick)
4 cups miniature marshmallows
1 tbs vanilla extract
6 cups Rice Krispie cereal (chocolate Cocoa Krispies were popular also)

DIRECTIONS
Thoroughly grease bottom and sides of 13"x9"x2" baking pan with butter, Crisco, or baking spray.

In large saucepan, melt the butter over very low heat. When the butter has melted, add the marshmallows. Cook, stirring constantly with a wooden spoon, until the marshmallows have completely dissolved. Stir in vanilla extract.

Turn the mixture out into large mixing bowl and add the cereal. (You can use either cereal alone or mix chocolate and regular variety.)

Mix well, and then press mixture into greased baking pan. Cool completely (you can speed up chilling process by putting into the refrigerator). Once cool and firm, cut the mixture into 2-inch bars. Remove the bars from the pan with spatula and transfer to plate. Bars can be individually wrapped in plastic for storage.

Kristen H was another of the Bridge students who had comfort and confidence in the kitchen. She also had the warm heart and patience that allowed her to work successfully with senior citizens. Her family did not understand that Kristen needed to find her own way to grow in the world. Because they had other goals for her, she was unable to use her talents to gain independence. But this soup demonstrated one of her areas of expertise.

SOUTHWESTERN VEGETABLE SOUP
6 to 8 servings

INGREDIENTS

3 tbs olive oil

1 cup chopped celery

1 cup chopped carrots

½ cup chopped onions

1 15-oz can black beans, drained

1 28-oz can chopped tomatoes, undrained

6 cups chicken broth (can use canned broth, or chicken stock or 6 cups of boiling water with 6-7 chicken bouillon cubes)

1 15-oz can corn kernels, drained

Few drops of hot pepper sauce, to taste (optional)

12 oz shredded cheddar cheese

DIRECTIONS:

Heat oil in stockpot. When oil is hot, add onion and sauté until tender but not brown. Add carrots and celery and cook all together until all the vegetables are tender.

Add beans and canned tomatoes with juice, and reduce temperature to simmer.

Add chicken broth and cook at low temperature for 20 minutes, stirring occasionally.

Add corn and hot sauce (if using).

Continue to simmer for 10 minutes.

Add shredded cheese to individual serving bowls before serving.

This tastes good served with guacamole, sour cream, and salsa with toasted tortillas or Frito chips.

To prepare guacamole: remove skin from very ripe avocado. Remove pit. Mash flesh with prepared salsa to taste.

This recipe was part of the end of the year holiday celebration hosted by Bridge and second-year Food Lab students. It was fun to prepare. Students realized that they could make the recipe, wrap it in small batches, and give them away as stocking stuffers or mini gifts or as an energy boost to get through the season.

HAPPY HOLIDAY DELIGHTS

INGREDIENTS
1 large box of Golden Grahams, or any type of Chex cereal
1 jar unsalted peanuts
1 cup raisins (optional)
1 large bar white chocolate or 1 bag white chocolate chips

DIRECTIONS
Cover large cookie sheet with wax paper.
Mix cereal, nuts, and raisins (if using) in large bowl.
Place chocolate in microwave-proof bowl or in saucepan.
Heat to melt; then pour immediately over cereal mixture.
Toss chocolate and cereal mix to blend well.
Spread out on prepared pan.
Place in refrigerator until firm.
Break mixture into chunks to serve or wrap.

Because one more Bridge student, Matt C, had a complicated medical history, he had never been encouraged to expand his range of potential vocational options. He came from a privileged background and was accustomed to having everything he wanted and needed. The Service Learning curriculum we followed in Bridge Year asked him to explore and try many new things. When he discovered that he could make his favorite cookies from scratch, he was thrilled. When he also learned that others shared his enthusiasm for his homemade cookies, he was inspired to return home and investigate starting a business producing the homemade goodies we had prepared and sold in our bake sale. He had never imagined that there might be a way for him to find some way to serve others while feeling satisfied with himself.

PEANUT BUTTER DELIGHTS
(approx. 48 cookies)
INGREDIENTS
2 cups flour
½ tsp baking soda
¼ tsp salt (use only if using unsalted butter)
1 cup butter, softened
1¼ cup brown sugar, firmly packed
1¼ cup white sugar
3 large eggs
2 tsp vanilla
1 cup creamy peanut butter

DIRECTIONS
Preheat oven to 350 degrees.

In medium bowl, sift together flour, baking soda, and salt (if using salted butter, eliminate extra salt).

In another bowl, using electric mixer, cream butter using medium speed. Gradually, add brown and white sugar until they are well mixed together. Add eggs and vanilla. Add peanut butter. Mix at low speed until light and fluffy. Add flour mixture slowly, and then mix together until combined.

Lightly grease cookie sheet.

Drop dough by rounded teaspoons onto baking sheet, leaving space between cookies. With wet fork, make crisscross marks on cookies.

Bake 9-11 minutes, until bottoms are golden brown. Leave on cookie sheet until firm (1-2 minutes), then transfer to rack to cool.

CHAPTER 5

MOTIVATION

One of the admission criteria for an applicant to the Threshold Program is that the student be motivated. How that motivation is defined, explained, and evidenced is mysterious. Some students appear motivated by being cheerful and optimistic about taking on a new adventure. Others appear motivated because they offer serious, thoughtful responses to questions about their plans for the future. Defining motivation has challenged educators for many years. A major study of motivation completed at the University of Southern Australia resulted in a workshop offered to students who were unsure of their direction. The following commentary is from this workshop:

> What is motivation? Motivation is a desire to achieve a goal, combined with the energy to work towards that goal. Students who are motivated have a desire to undertake their study and complete the requirements of their course."

Are you a motivated student? Being a motivated student doesn't mean you are always excited or fully committed to your study, but it does mean you will complete the tasks set for you even when assignments or practicals are difficult, or seem uninteresting.

Positive and Negative Motivation

Sometimes a distinction is made between positive and negative motivation. Positive motivation is a response that includes enjoyment and optimism about the tasks you are involved in. Negative motivation involves undertaking tasks because there will be undesirable outcomes, e.g. failing a subject, if tasks are not completed. Almost all students will experience positive and negative motivation, as well as loss of motivation, at different times during their life at university. What seems to work best for most people is to understand that both positive and negative motivation is useful, and that sometimes students will need to search for motivation."

Reading this study was helpful but didn't completely resolve my quandary about figuring out why and how to judge and develop motivation in Threshold students.

Even for those students admitted to Threshold whose motivation was at least acceptable to pass through the interview process and who made it through their first year at Threshold, some demonstrated inconsistency in their desire to focus on schoolwork and complete assignments at their highest level. As faculty members, we were sometimes unsure how to inspire and activate some students primarily because their level of engagement in various classes was so irregular. Taking into account the wide array of learning styles and cognitive ability could not always explain why certain students were so challenged in some classes and successful in others. We made every effort to understand these differences so that we could accommodate and help the students perform at the appropriate level. All the second-year students were assigned to my Food Lab. There were some who displayed the inconsistent level of engagement that they did in other classes in the beginning of the year; some were not completely reliable about their attendance or their punctuality, and their involvement in the classroom activity varied widely. However, as the semester developed, most weeks even some of the least reliable students tended to attend this class.

Although it is difficult to be objective about colleagues who are sincere, considerate, well trained, experienced, and enthusiastic about their teaching, I know that the Threshold faculty makes every possible effort to offer students the best possible learning environment. So how can we understand why the same student who does not attend many other classes, or who won't contribute to class discussions in most classes, manages to make it to Food Lab each week and puts effort and enthusiasm into his/her assignment in class? I know it is not because I am such an exciting and stimulating teacher. I wonder if Maslow's principle of the hierarchy of needs is a factor in their engagement in this class. Maybe, without being even slightly aware of this factor, could it possibly be true that the most basic need for survival, food, is a factor? It is hard for me to believe that the answer is so simplistic. Is it maybe because there is no homework assignments, other than the essential requirement that they deliver the recipes that they want to cook? Or does the fact that they take turns as the class leader provide a comfortable level of competition? Or does the food that we prepare taste so much better than the food in the campus dining facilities?

John Dewey (1859-1952), an esteemed philosopher and educator, might have provided some answers to my question. He believed that education is life itself. He said: "We learn by doing, if we reflect on what we have done." He thought that learning was active and schooling unnecessarily long and restrictive. His idea was that children came to school to do things and live in a community, which gave them real, guided experiences, which fostered their capacity to contribute to society. For example, Dewey believed that students should be involved in real-life tasks and challenges. He said "maths could be learnt via learning proportions in cooking or figuring out how long it would take to get from one place to another by mule." He said "history could be learnt by experiencing how people lived, geography, what the climate was like, and how plants and animals grew." Maybe Dewey's theory could account for some of the factors that made attendance more consistent in this class.

I have certainly noticed the value of learning by experience. Several students had "a-ha" experiences transferring four ¼-cup measuring cups into a 1-cup measure. Suddenly, the concept of "one-quarter cup" meant something. Fractions became much more tangible. We discussed how many 1/3-cup measuring cups went into a one-cup measure, and practiced with measuring cups and spoons. Suddenly the concept of dividing material into pieces was visible. Even if this were not the very first time they that they had participated in this mini-experiment, it was empowering for some of the students to be able to comprehend what had once been just a mathematical term that might have felt somewhat threatening and frightening.

For some students with learning challenges, math represented one of the areas that set them apart from their peers. Some had almost shut down and claimed that math was too difficult for them to comprehend. Since arithmetic and numbers were definitely not my strong suit, I could relate to these fears. I was able to demonstrate how much more visible and real math could be when they could see the results of their measuring. For other students whose learning difficulties were more word than number based, cooking also provided motivation to try to get the meaning of the words we used. Color-coded measuring cups and spoons were visual tools to see the differences between teaspoons and tablespoons, and made it simpler to identify which cup/spoon was called for in a recipe.

Learning to bake with yeast was a good example of learning by experience. Since it also took patience, there were many elements that contributed to the pleasure of making dough. Reading the recipe carefully came first. Then testing the water to see that it was exactly the right temperature took practice. The idea that water at "body temperature" really meant feeling the difference when you sprinkled water on the underside of your wrist was a new concept. Checking to be sure that the yeast culture was alive forced the students to watch and wait until the mixture bubbled. I explained that baking with yeast was similar to caring for an infant. Warmth, food, and shelter were essential for both the baby's and the dough's growth. Adding the sugar to the yeast mix and watching it bubble was informative. Beginning to gradually incorporate flour illustrated many of the issues we were exploring. The temperature in the room, the humidity, and other factors determined exactly how much flour was needed, that day, in that room. Students had to learn to listen to the dough, and give respect to the mixture before adding more flour. When they learned to knead and stretch the ball of dough and see if it could support its own weight, they realized that the dough was speaking to them. Putting the dough aside to rise, and then punching it down when it grew, were all part of the experiment. Tasting the bread, buns, or cake they created offered the best grading system. The aroma, sweet taste, and creamy texture of well-risen dough told them everything about how well they had accomplished their assignment.

For students who did not come with a family cooking history, learning to read and follow recipe directions was foreign. For others who had enjoyed standing next to their grandmother as they cooked or baked together, the process was more familiar. However, there were many grandmas who cooked from tradition with a pinch of this and a pinch of that. In terms of taste and flavor, that traditional approach certainly worked, but in terms of learning to live independently it was important to gain some concept of gathering and using information from common resources. Whatever the background, cooking had an intrinsic motivating force that made learning more valuable.

Danielle offered a great example to witness some of the motivating factors in cooking. She was a wonderful natural cook. There were many reasons why she enjoyed Food Lab and was so eager to perform in this class. It would be difficult for me to prioritize the factors, and I doubt that she would find that an easy task either. She really enjoyed food and that might have been most important. She also valued attention, and felt pride in her comfort in the kitchen as it offered a means of getting a positive response from others. She also had a strong family tradition of enjoying food. Preparing food, serving others, and eating were all sources of pleasurable memories. The additional element of gaining praise and compliments for her food creations was a bonus. There was something else that might have impacted on her interest in this class. Danielle had a complicated reading disorder, which had frustrated her throughout her life. Although she was highly functional in certain areas, she had to fight to gain knowledge in traditional ways. She started to make good use of adaptive technology, but still enjoyed demonstrating her ability to perform in a tangible, convenient way. Her ease in the kitchen and the delicious recipes she produced were concrete evidence of her real abilities. Learning by doing and gaining knowledge through experience was definitely her preferred method of operation.

What made cooking work for Danielle was the opportunity to mimic her family members as they prepared the tasty selections. Her meatballs were succulent and juicy. She was proud to demonstrate her competence using her stored memories.

DANIELLE'S HOMEMADE MARINARA AND MEATBALLS
Serves 8

INGREDIENTS

Sauce
1 tbs olive oil
3-4 cloves garlic, minced
2 8-oz cans crushed tomatoes
1 tbs fresh basil, chopped, or 1 tsp. dried basil flakes
¼ cup grated parmesan cheese
4-6 baby carrots, chopped fine
Salt/pepper to taste

Meatballs
2 lbs ground beef (or ground turkey)
4 eggs
4 cloves garlic, minced
1 tbs chopped fresh parsley or 1 tsp. dried parsley flakes
½ cup bread crumbs

DIRECTIONS:
Begin preparing sauce before cooking meatballs so sauce has time to develop flavor. Sauce can be prepared the day before and refrigerated overnight.

Heat heavy saucepan over medium heat. Place olive oil in pan, them sauté garlic until soft but not brown. Add all remaining ingredients. Stir and simmer while preparing meatballs.

Preheat oven to 350 degrees.

Mix all meatball ingredients together. Roll into small or medium balls. Place on lightly greased cookie sheet. Bake 10-12 minutes, stirring occasionally.

Remove meatballs from oven. If sauce has been in refrigerator, heat sauce till simmering. Gently place meatballs into sauce and simmer all together for additional 10-15 minutes. Serve over cooked pasta. Sprinkle with grated parmesan cheese if desired.

In my attempt to try to examine why people enjoyed cooking, I looked to other experts besides Maslow and Dewey. Steven Reiss from Ohio State University completed a study of six thousand people. He then proposed a theory that sixteen basic desires guided human behavior. As I studied his model, I recognized that many of the factors that he identified were consistent with the goals and practices of Food Lab.

The following list was taken directly from Steven Reiss's model.

Acceptance, the need for approval

This factor is certainly a part of most student/teacher relationships. For many young adults with learning disabilities, the need for acceptance, especially from someone in an academic leadership position, can be complicated. For some, who attempted to move out of special-education classes into more of the mainstream curriculum, it could be a struggle to gain acceptance from both the teacher and the other students. For those students who stayed in contained classes where they might have received specialized programming, the need for acceptance from the greater population in the high school was a constant battle. Although most of the students felt more comfortable and better understood once they enrolled in the Threshold Program, the need for acceptance might have continued as a habit, if not an actual need. Students exhibited an array of behaviors that they adopted to find approval, some more effective and appropriate than others. Producing a tasty meal almost always delivered the positive feedback and approval that everyone wants and needs.

Curiosity, the need to think

Although there was some initial concern among some of the students, especially those who did not come from a cooking tradition, most of the students were curious and excited about the possibility of being able to prepare food on their own. The students in previous years' classes had told them about the kind of foods they would cook, the cookbook they would produce at the end of the year, and the celebrations they would host. The idea of thinking, planning, and seeing direct results from their efforts was intriguing to most of the class members. Cooking also took advantage of the ability to think or problem-solve using a wider array of senses. Some students, especially those who had some previous history with cooking, at home or in another program, were creative with the use of spices and flavorings. Using taste or smell, they could turn an average meal into a more flavorful option. This ability inspired other students to think and express curiosity about reading a recipe and making changes to adjust to their own style or taste preference. This idea certainly motivated some students to explore beyond the basic ingredients the recipe indicated. Trying to duplicate some of the tastes of foods they enjoyed in restaurants enticed some students. It was empowering when someone asked a chef for a recipe or researched a flavor that they particularly enjoyed and we were able to reproduce a facsimile of the wonderful taste they remembered.

Eating, the need for food

We learned from Maslow's hierarchy that the need for food and survival is most basic. The more complex need to prepare food satisfied another level of need. In this class, I believe it was the combination of learning to satisfy many needs at an increasingly complex level that was most fulfilling. The fact that they were exposed to a broad array of foods prepared with friends may have been a factor. Fulfilling many needs, including curiosity and acceptance, might have led some students to sample foods that they had never tasted before. Because we discussed nutrition and tried to analyze the basic food groups in every meal, students were also learning to adapt food to their own preferences and needs. Whether it was low-calorie, low-fat, low carbohydrates, peanut-free, allergy proof, or whatever, it was interesting to see how the students got into the puzzle of figuring out how to make substitutions to comply with their own individual taste and health requirements while still meeting the basic need to have the food they needed and enjoyed.

Family, the need to raise children

Food Lab was not directly connected to any long range family planning goals; however the students were well aware that before they could consider themselves full, independent, responsible adults they would need some ability to plan and prepare meals. As we discussed nutrition and basic menu planning, we included the various essential food groups. Students knew, from their courses about child growth and development, how important nutrition was to the physical and mental needs of children. With the current focus on obesity, we discussed how students could learn to take better control of the quantity and quality of foods they consumed. Being able to manage their own diet allowed them to project to the time when they might be responsible for a partner or child's healthy eating habits.

We also discussed the social significance of mealtime for family and group communication. We talked about the adage "the way to a man's heart is through his stomach." Although there was some discussion about whether this concept really worked anymore, there was general agreement, that both males and females would appreciate developing a relationship with someone who could prepare a decent meal.

Honor, the need to be loyal to the traditional values of one's clan/ethnic group

Because the students were encouraged to share family recipes, in many cases, this class provided an opportunity to reveal, examine, and discuss their ethnic roots. While preparing and eating traditional foods from their cultural history, they had the chance to display pride and loyalty to their roots. Some students learned more about their own family as they searched for recipes. For some students, eating food from another culture made them question their roots and wonder about the source of certain recipes in their own family repertoire of favorite foods.

Idealism, the need for social justice

I had not planned to explore or focus on broader social needs as a basic premise of this class, but, as we were eating our meal, I encouraged and sometimes initiated the opportunity to share thoughts and feelings about things going on in the world. This was not designed to be a current events class, but issues like famine or deprivation of any basic need were natural conversation themes at the dining table. There was no direct pressure to express any specific opinion, or even to be particularly well informed about any topic. Many heated and healthy discussions developed, which may have opened some eyes and minds. It was exciting to observe someone absorb a new fact or perspective about an issue that they may have never previously even considered.

Because some students had family members serving in the military, it was natural to talk about the meals their siblings or parents were eating. We learned about both their rations and the local foods in the areas where they were deployed. A few students had traveled with their families while in the military and had experienced living and dining in other countries. This usually broadened their food tastes and preferences. It was less complicated to share eating habits than political issues, while still getting an image for a different way of life.

Independence, the need for individuality

One of the primary goals of The Threshold Program is to help the students develop independent living skills before they graduate. This class was designed to directly contribute to this goal. It was possible to consider Food Lab as assisting in the development of independence in both definitions. It served as both a means to teach students to care for one of their basic needs, and also to help them explore and develop their own food preferences and eating styles. Because students came from a variety of backgrounds, they were exposed to new flavors, and they also learned about different ways in which families provided for the dietary needs. For some people, eating in restaurants and/or ordering take-out food was a rarity, while for others, their family prepared home cooked meals from scratch on a less frequent schedule. Students learned from one another as they realized these differences. I reassured them that although there was no one right or wrong way to get their nourishment, it was important to recognize and respect the different ways that people went about feeding the family. This also was a starting point for discussions about finding ways to achieve healthy eating from fast food, and considering the diverse ways in which people chose to spend their money. Analyzing a menu from a fast food restaurant to find a well-balanced meal was an interesting project. There were definitely some groans and indications of surprise when people realized the number of calories, amount of cholesterol, etc., that went into even a Happy Meal.

Order, the need for organized, stable, predictable environments

Maintaining order and a stable, predictable environment is essential in the kitchen. So that someone can easily see what ingredients are available before one can begin to follow a recipe, it is essential that the cupboards be well organized. Checking if we had enough milk, butter, vegetable oil, sugar, etc., was a big part of preparing the shopping list. Knowing that we could count on the flour being in the right canister and the soy sauce on the shelf in the refrigerator door kept people comfortable. Unloading the dishwasher and returning the plates and glasses to their assigned location, made setting the table much more efficient. It was relieving, even for those students whose dorm rooms were more chaotic, to know that our kitchen was neat and clean. Those students who had the need to maintain structure in their environment in order to focus on their work were able to feel more comfortable when they assisted the other students and me, the teacher, to encourage sanitation and order in the kitchen. Even those students who rarely saw the need for order in their environment and found it unique to see value in returning things to their regularly assigned location, were quite surprised to see how much easier it was to take on a project in the kitchen when they knew exactly where each ingredient and utensil was located. The predictability of the schedule in each class was also reassuring to some students. Although the finished product of each meal might be a surprise, the process of getting the food to the table was predictable and comforting.

Some students were unsure of who they wanted to be. Trying to find their role and their comfort zone took some time. Greg, a tall, good looking young man, presented himself as a bit of a tough guy. He was a natural leader, but he rarely revealed his tender, gentler side until he came to Food Lab. He was an excellent cook, who enjoyed eating healthy, natural food. His need for organization and structure was a great match for the whole cooking process. He also occasionally demonstrated compassion for those students who didn't have the same comfort in the kitchen. He didn't reveal this attribute consistently, but it demonstrated that finding this "island" did allow him to show his core values.

NUTRITIOUS AND DELICIOUS EGG BEATER'S OMELET
Serves 2-3 generously
INGREDIENTS
2 cartons of Egg Beaters of your choice (or 3 regular large eggs, beaten)

1 small onion, peeled and chopped fine (¾ cup chopped onion)

¾ cup chopped red pepper

Any other vegetables that you prefer can be added (such as chopped mushrooms or zucchini)

1 cup shredded cheese

Salsa or ketchup to taste

Salt/pepper

DIRECTIONS
Spray large skillet with baking spray.

Heat pan and pour in Egg Beaters, or beaten eggs.

Add chopped vegetables. Cook together, scrapping pan to be sure that eggs and vegetables are being evenly cooked. Sprinkle cheese over top. Cook until cheese is melted.

Spoon onto plates.

Serve with salsa or ketchup.

Toasted whole wheat English muffins are a tasty addition to meal.

Physical activity, the need for exercise

Although the common perception of the fat, jolly chef, or the Pillsbury doughboy might be recognizable in the media, these images are not always valid anymore. Anyone engaged in meal preparation realizes that cooking and baking are good exercise. Buying food, unloading the groceries, stocking the shelves, measuring, stirring, kneading, are physical tasks. Students were occasionally surprised to see how much energy putting a meal on the table actually took. It seemed more reasonable to indulge in eating a cookie after baking it from scratch rather than exert the more limited energy to open a package of store-bought goodies. The fact that cooking took physical stamina, as well as mental acuity, was enlightening.

Power, the need for influence of will

Being "head chef," when the student had the chance to select the menu and take leadership of the cooking process, was a power trip, in a very positive way. Even those students, who usually were not perceived as leaders to others, or more importantly to themselves, were required to take charge in at least one class. Some students needed encouragement to even select a recipe. However, once the cooking process began, some natural leaders, at least in the kitchen, emerged. Several students who tended to be quiet or even vacant in other classes revealed a secret ability or interest in cooking. Watching someone like Andrew or Zach demonstrate confidence and pride in their culinary skills was amazing. The same young men who tended to lag behind or go about their business in a shy, quiet way in other class's demonstrated pride and comfort in this setting. I was pleased to see them take charge in an area that no one had recognized or anticipated. We also learned for the first time that several students had culinary training in high school or in some other training facility. Here was an untapped area of skills and leadership opportunities that had never before been acknowledged. Seeing their pride and satisfaction was pleasurable for the students, their peers and the instructor.

Cooking prowess was also a less competitive means to demonstrate influence and power than athletics. In this circumstance, everyone was a winner and the leader or leaders had the chance to serve others and share his/her talent. The head chef, the sous chef, the dishwasher, and everyone who took part in the preparation each had a significant role and could enjoy the product together. This "power trip" happened each week on a scheduled basis and included every class member. Realizing that the stars of the Food Channel had become icons and popular heroes interested some of the class members.

Romance, the need for sex

Although we have heard the statement "Food is love." of all the sixteen basic needs identified by Reiss as factors in intrinsic motivation, I must admit that this was one of them that did not quite fit into my initial premise. Initially, I found it challenging to identify how Food Lab fulfilled needs for romance or sex. With a stretch of imagination, it might be possible to see how in the future, someone might use their cooking skills to entice someone to follow them home for a home-cooked meal. Everyone knows that it is much easier to fall in love with a full stomach, but it did not seem to be one of the motivating forces behind this class! One could conceive of the possibility that someone, doing a bit of research, would find some aphrodisiac additive to brownies that could turn a partner on. However, this was really not one of the goals of this class. We could also acknowledge the possibility that caring for someone by providing good nutrition and sustenance certainly was an expression of affection, but it was the more sensuous aspect that was difficult to imagine. But then I realize that in advertisements, the picture of a glamorous couple sitting in an intimate setting in an elegant restaurant sipping wine to accompany their extravagant meal is symbolic of the courtship ritual, so maybe there is more to this factor than I initially recognized.

Saving, the need to collect

If one compared the value of buying food in a restaurant to preparing a similar meal at home, cooking usually won that battle. For someone on a budget, it was usually easier to save some money by planning basic meals and shopping carefully. If someone was creative and thoughtful about using the ingredients purchased for one meal, there were usually ways to extend some of the food that one bought for one recipe for use in another. Collecting recipes and other meal ideas also became a force for some students. Seeing the cookbook that was produced each year was obvious proof of their efforts and demonstrated that measure of motivation and pride.

Krystal was proud to demonstrate her cooking competence and confidence. Because she had many responsibilities at home, she was often the prime cook for her family. She did not share many of the economic advantages that other students brought to Threshold. She had to work a bit harder to establish her place. She was expert at finding recipes that she could prepare without spending much too much time and money. This recipe can be served unstuffed as basic French toast. When stuffed it makes a multi-purpose meal-for breakfast, brunch, lunch, or dinner. Adding some sautéed vegetables or a salad makes a complete, healthy meal.

FANCY STUFFED FRENCH TOAST
Serves 3-4 but can be doubled etc to serve as many as necessary

INGREDIENTS
6 eggs
1 cup low fat milk or water
Margarine or butter for greasing griddle or skillet
Loaf of sliced white or wheat bread

Optional for stuffing:
Sliced ham
Sliced cheddar, American, or Swiss cheese

DIRECTIONS:
In medium shallow bowl, scramble together eggs and milk or water.

Heat griddle or skillet until drops of water bead on surface. Add tablespoon butter or margarine and cook until melts.

Holding bread on fork, dip into egg mixture until moist all over.

Toast bread on hot griddle until browned and firm. Have patience to wait until bread is well cooked before flipping to second side. When ready, flip to other side and cook until firm.

Bread is now ready to serve with syrup or sugar as regular French toast.

To stuff:

Place sliced ham and cheese on warm bread; squeeze together and return to skillet to melt cheese and merge all flavors.

Serve warm.

Social contact, the need for friends (peer relationships)

This class, perhaps because it was perceived as less competitive and demanding, was an opportunity for social relationships to develop. Students who had never given certain classmates the opportunity to prove themselves in other social situations, sometimes learned new things about one another in this environment. Sometimes, the reputation or social understanding that students developed of one another changed dramatically when put into a different context. Another consequence of Food Lab was developing an entirely different view of a person than one usually perceived in other situations. For some students, the only means that had developed before coming to Threshold to gather attention was negative attention-seeking behavior. Many students were unaware of their own value or talent. They remembered only being victimized or being critical of others. It was wonderful to see several of the students use their ability to prepare food as a means of getting positive feedback. Developing relationships was more likely when they were able to demonstrate a definable talent that was interesting and desirable in a friend. Being a good cook and a willing participant in food prep and sanitation seemed a better way to develop relationships than the negative behavior that these particular young people demonstrated more often.

Another social consequence of this class was demonstrated in Liz, whose well-developed set of armor left her unable to take many risks. One of my most vibrant memories was of this young lady, who had a very narrow frame of acceptable foods and was quite rigid in her willingness to sample new flavors, textures, or spice. She used her food preferences in a dramatic, attention-seeking manner. One day, Liz decided to comply with one of the basic parameters of the class: to try one bite of any food to which she had no prohibition. She had never eaten a chicken drumstick in her whole life, but because one of her best friends chose this recipe, Liz's need for acceptance and social contact was primary when she took the first bite. It was the second and third bites that opened her world. When she completed eating her second drumstick, her next impulse was to call home and tell her mother about the exciting adventure she had undertaken.

There were so many examples when students had never given one another the opportunity to be viewed as potential friends. Sometimes they learned when cooking and eating together that some element they might have overlooked that might be a connection between them. Perhaps, even something as basic as sharing a preference for one food over another, like enjoying Hawaiian pizza, could become a common ground.

Status, the need for social standing/importance

For many students, because academics had never been the area where they gained status or even approval, finding a course where their attributes could be considered important or worthy of gaining social standing was unique. Because the ability to cook drew upon so many different areas of ability, there were many more opportunities for a student to shine in this class. Mike really liked to cook and eat and had a solid background in food preparation skills. He contributed many recipes and led the class with pride as he shared his knowledge. He became one of the "go to" members when other students were not as confident in their skill development. He liked being someone who was able to assist another person who was not as comfortable with one of the techniques we tried. He knew how to use all the equipment and was helpful in demonstrating certain skills that others found confusing. Mike also knew how to use knives safely and was willing to help others who were more cautious and less confident using sharp knives. For David, who was shy and uncomfortable having attention drawn to him, his love of international foods was a natural draw in this class. He liked to share less common recipes and was willing to discuss his travels and experiences eating and learning about foods in other countries. This was a means for him to establish some social standing that didn't require him to do anything extraordinary or difficult. He gained some importance and also gained the ability to eat some of his favorite foods. Dan was another example of a student who had difficulty establishing relationships in other classes. His recipe for General Gao's chicken was a good example of someone gaining status by just sharing their unique knowledge. This recipe was one that was considered complicated and special to those people who liked Chinese food. Dan shared a recipe and helped prepare a meal that could compare favorably with any restaurant. He achieved a standing in the class that was remembered throughout the year.

If only Dan could display the same competence and confidence when he was doing other things that he did when he was head chef. When he selected this recipe and took leadership, he was initially unsure that he could prepare it. He loved eating this recipe at a local restaurant and tried to find a way to closely duplicate the flavors. We managed to make a sticky, sweet, delectable dish similar to that served at the neighborhood Asian restaurant. Dan's pride was evident and he became sociable and positive in that class.

DELECTABLE GENERAL GAO'S CHICKEN
Serves 4

INGREDIENTS
1 lb boneless, skinless chicken breasts (approximately 4 large half breasts)

¼ cup flour to dredge chicken

2 tbs vegetable oil (or peanut oil)

¼ cup sugar

¼ cup unsweetened pineapple juice

¼ cup light soy sauce

¼ cup white distilled vinegar

2 cloves garlic, peeled and crushed

1 tsp fresh ginger, finely grated

¼ tsp cayenne pepper

1 tbs cornstarch, mixed with 1 tbs cold water (or more to correct consistency)

3 green onions cut into ¼ inch pieces

Steamed white rice and julienned carrots to accompany meal

DIRECTIONS
Trim chicken of all fat and cartilage. Cut into bite-sized pieces.

Dredge chicken in flour by shaking together in plastic bag until chicken is lightly coated.

Heat oil over medium heat in wok or deep skillet. Stir-fry chicken until golden brown.

Combine sauce ingredients (sugar, pineapple juice, soy sauce, vinegar, garlic, and ginger) and warm over low heat.

Remove chicken from skillet or wok and sprinkle with cayenne pepper. Add sauce to skillet and stir until well mixed and sugar is dissolved. Add cornstarch mixture and stir until sauce is thickened. Return chicken to wok; add green onions. Stir all together.

Serve with rice and carrots, if desired.

Tranquility, the need to be safe

This desire represented another unintended consequence of Food Lab. Perhaps the class felt like a haven for those students who had some prior experience or comfort in the kitchen. For others who enjoyed cooking with their families, being in the kitchen might have reflected some warm and peaceful reminders. It also was a place where everyone had an equal footing. Whatever their major field of study, wherever they planned to live in the future, everyone would have to eat and probably would want to learn the basics of food preparation. There was some safety in sharing these goals.

Vengeance, the need to strike back

No matter how hard I try to come up with some slight connection, it is too challenging for me to conceive of a way that Food Lab provided a means for vengeance. We did not have any "Iron Chef" competitions, nor did we rank any meal over any other. My goal each week was to emphasize the tranquility, acceptance, order, independence, and curiosity needs. Any others that were satisfied were a bonus. Vengeance did not enter the picture.

Even though vengeance might not have been a factor to help this class rank as a perfect example of Stephen Reiss's model for intrinsic motivation and his sixteen basic desires theory, I believe that fifteen out of sixteen or ninety-four percent might rank as a good explanation for the attendance and positive attitude that Food Lab generated each year.

CHAPTER 6

CONNECTION TO HERITAGE AND TRADITIONS

For many students, and particularly for those with learning differences, finding similarities with peers is important. In many elementary schools, the youngsters do some research to identity elements of their heritage. Once they reach middle school, they tend to try to bury their differences and search for common grounds. Food can be a bond for students when they cook together and realize the similarities rather than differences in their backgrounds. Educators could use cooking classes to bring students together over shared food traditions or tastes. For many of the Threshold students, a need and desire to fit in and to establish common ground with peers was important. Because of their struggles with academic work, they often felt different than their classmates. In their past, unless they were fortunate enough to find a commonality, like playing a sport or singing in a chorus with other students in their school, a certain amount of discrimination or negative stereotyping was frequently part of their background. In order to feel more similar to their classmates, many students wanted to hide or minimize any unique factors in their background or family life. Even special features, which they might treasure privately, could not be identified or exaggerated, if they were not exactly like the traditions and histories that matched the majority of their peers. In Food Lab, when encouraged to share recipes or cooking habits that their parents, grandparents, or other relatives had prepared for or with them, initially some students were reluctant. It usually took some encouragement in the beginning of the year to convince someone to bring in an example of the culturally unique recipes that they cooked and ate with their family.

Arielle had a particularly complex and fascinating mixture of traditions. She grew up in the United States. She knew that she was the beloved adopted daughter with Indian heritage in a Jewish American family. Her mother was eager to give Arielle pride in both her Jewish rituals and some of the culture from her native India. When preparing potato latkes, one of her favorite Chanukah memories, Arielle enjoyed participating in cooking and eating the crispy pancakes and displayed comfort and familiarity with the traditional food. But when it was time to share her own recipe, she shyly asked if she could make food from her birth heritage, samosas and lassis. Because I was not at all familiar with preparing these dishes, I asked Arielle if she had ever prepared these delicious treats. She replied that although she had never cooked either of those dishes, a new friend, another young woman with Indian heritage, who was enrolled in the regular Lesley University undergraduate program, expressed willingness to cooperate with us and try to find recipes and cook the dishes together. Here was a wonderful opportunity to expand horizons in multiple ways. Not only would Arielle fulfill her assignment and take her turn as head chef, she would introduce the other students to some foods with which they had little, if any, experience. We, as a class and representatives of a program, would get acquainted with a student that many of the Threshold students might have seen around campus but had no means to connect with. We experienced another "win-win" opportunity. The samosas were delicious and easy to prepare. We never quite managed to get the lassis to work, but we had lots of fun trying. Here was a good illustration of group dynamics when we learned that there was a group of students on campus who seemed different and maybe even strange, but were really not all that different and strange, once some common ground was established.

As an international adoptee, Arielle had a complex background. She wanted and needed to reconnect with the heritage of her birth family. Through food, she found the connection to her history. It also allowed her to make some friends who shared her heritage. She was so pleased to prepare something that tasted so good and introduced a part of her that had been unknown to her friends. Her pride in tracing her roots and using this part of her background to establish new relationships was evident.

ARIELLE'S SUPER SAMOSAS
12-14 samosas

INGREDIENTS
½ tsp turmeric
¼ tsp dried coriander
½ tsp cumin powder
Several slices of fresh ginger root, peeled and minced or grated
Salt
1 large onion, peeled and chopped
1 tbs vegetable oil
3 large potatoes, peeled and chopped into bite-sized pieces
3 large carrots, peeled and chopped into bite-sized pieces
2 cups frozen peas, thawed
2 cloves garlic, peeled and minced
1 lime
Few leaves of fresh coriander, if desired
Oil for frying
One package egg roll wrappers (can use tortillas cut into quarters)

DIRECTIONS
Mix all spices and ginger.
Brown chopped onion in 1 tbs oil in skillet.
Once onion is soft, add carrots and potatoes, and sauté all together until tender but not mushy. Add peas, then spice mixture and about ½ cup water. Cover pan and let simmer together on low heat for 10-25 minutes until all vegetables are soft and liquid is reduced.
Sprinkle mixture with lime juice. Add coriander if using.

Cut wrappers or tortillas into semi circles. Fold wrappers into cone shape. Fill each with 1-2 tbs vegetable filling. Seal edges by dampening edges with bit of water.

Heat oil in skillet. Fry samosas at low temperature until soft. Drain and serve. Can be eaten warm or cold.

Claire was atypical even for a Threshold student. Although she was not the first student with Down syndrome to be admitted to the program, she had some areas of strength and interest that were unique. She had an enormous affection and interest in the arts. Her long-range goals were also out of the ordinary for our population. She wanted to be a writer or director of theater productions. Written assignments were not among her favorite activities, but writing journals, stories, or short plays was a mission for Claire. Something else that was precious to her in a Jewish American family was her connection to the Jamaican Islands. Here was a blonde Caucasian young lady from Wisconsin who was very eager to share her knowledge and pride in the traditions of Jamaica. She was unsure how to share this part of her history. It was in the kitchen that it all came together. Claire asked to reproduce the recipes that her Jamaican housekeeper, with whom she had a strong bond, had taught her. Because this woman gave her love, support, and confidence, Claire blossomed when sharing the recipes and stories of her upbringing. Her classmates had a glimpse into Claire's background and precious memories that had not been previously revealed. Eating johnny cakes and fried plantains was a great way to learn.

CORNMEAL JOHNNY CAKES
Serves 8

INGREDIENTS
1 cup white cornmeal
Dash of salt
1 tsp. sugar
1 c. boiling water
1 egg, beaten
Milk
Shortening, butter, or vegetable oil

DIRECTIONS
Put cornmeal into mixing bowl. Add salt and sugar. Make a well in center of mixture. Pour in water to scald mixture. Let stand for a few minutes. Beat in egg.

Thin batter by adding milk until reaches thin consistency like pancake batter. Mix all together well.

Heat griddle or skillet until hot. Place butter or vegetable oil on pan. Spread over surface. Drop batter into pan. Cook completely on one side until browned and bubbly, then flip over and cook other side.

Johnny cakes taste good served with fried plantains.

FRIED PLANTAINS
INGREDIENTS

2-4 ripe plantains (look for them right next to bananas in market) Choose plantains that have some yellow color on skin, which makes them ready to cook

Vegetable oil for frying.

DIRECTIONS

Peel plantains. Slice diagonally into ½ inch pieces.

Coat bottom of skillet with thin layer of oil. Heat oil. Cook plantain slices until soft and lightly browned. Flip over and cook other side. Watch them carefully so they don't overcook. Takes 5-10 minutes to complete cooking.

Drain on paper towel before serving.

Isaac offered another example of a student who did not share ownership of his heritage easily. Because he came to Threshold from a private high school serving a similar population to the Threshold Program, he arrived on campus comfortable with living away from his family. He was a quiet young man who didn't speak up easily. It was difficult to get to know him, as he tended to merge into groups rather than assert himself and stand out in any way. He was one of the less eager volunteers to be head chef. Each week, with some coercion and coaching, Isaac did his part in preparing the meal and cleaning up, but he rarely commented on his favorite foods. Close to the end of the first semester, he knew that the time was almost up to do his share. He shyly asked if he could cook something from his Peruvian heritage. When I eagerly agreed to help him find an appropriate recipe, he mentioned saltado, a spicy beef dish. We did some research and asked his parents for assistance. As he began to describe the dish to the other students and chop the ingredients, a very different, more confident and capable Isaac emerged. The dish was simple to prepare, tasted delicious, and offered a great opportunity for Isaac to describe a bit more about his family and their traditions. Would we have ever learned about this part of his background or had the chance to see Isaac as a leader, even for a short time, without Food Lab? Here was a platform to share and to shine. Isaac rose to the occasion and beamed throughout the class.

Although some families incorporate their ethnic traditions and culture into their lives on a regular basis, there are others who choose not to infuse their daily life with their historic background. Sometimes students get only hints on their origins in some of the foods that the families enjoy cooking and eating. Isaac rarely spoke about his Peruvian heritage. He was unsure about sharing this recipe, but while we ate the spicy stew, he began to talk about his grandparents and his visits to Peru. Everyone learned about having respect for the hot peppers. Including at least one tablespoon of the diced jalapeno was essential, but people for who hotter is better can increase the dose.

PERUVIAN LOMO SALTADO
Serves 3 or 4

INGREDIENTS
1½ cup potato, peeled and chopped
2 tbs vegetable oil
½ cup thinly sliced onion
2 cloves garlic, peeled and minced
½ cup bell pepper, red or yellow, chopped
1 tbs jalapeno pepper, diced
½ lb sirloin steak, sliced thin
1 tomato, chopped
1 tsp fresh oregano or ½ tsp dried oregano
Salt and pepper, to taste

REMEMBER: jalapeno peppers are very spicy. Use rubber gloves when touching peppers and don't touch face or eyes after touching jalapenos. Keep hot peppers separate before cooking.

DIRECTIONS
Place large pot of water on stove, add a pinch of salt, and set to boil. When boiling, add potatoes and boil for 10-12 minutes, until potatoes are soft but not mushy. Remove and drain. Store in cold water until ready to use.

Heat oil in nonstick skillet. Sauté onion, garlic, and bell peppers. Add cooked potatoes and stir occasionally. Cook together until potato starts to brown.

Add jalapeno pepper and then steak. Sauté for few minutes until meat reaches right temperature/texture for your taste. (It is usually served medium rare)

Stir in tomato, oregano, salt and pepper. Serve warm.

This dish is often served over steamed rice.

Ethan had an unusually intense need to demonstrate his competence. As a tall, good-looking, sociable young man, he tended to attract attention and he had an established relationship with another popular female student. He had the potential to handle the academic curriculum but tended to neglect his assignments. Although he demonstrated evidence of his ability to comprehend the work in class, his reluctance to do his homework reduced his participation in class discussions. He covered up with an attitude implying that he didn't care about the work. His attendance in many classes was inconsistent and when he did show up, he was either late or had a reason why he had to leave before class time was up. It was a pleasant surprise to see Ethan in Food Lab. Most often, he was an eager, engaged student with well-developed food prep skills. He wanted to demonstrate one of his areas of competence and was willing to help the other students who were not as experienced as he was chopping or sautéing food. He submitted several recipes that were based on his Lithuanian ancestry. He remembered baking one recipe for an apple cake with his grandmother, describing how she would scrape her knuckles as she grated the apples and how hard she had to work to prepare food for the family. We were all pleased to recognize that with our modern conveniences, like a food processor, we could shred the apples with no pain whatsoever. We achieved the same results and Ethan felt great pride in producing a delicious cake that has become one of my new favorite baking treats.

Ethan struggled to get to many of his classes, in a down period in his life, but usually attended every Food Lab session. He did not perform at his optimal level, but he did come to class and provide support to the other students. After graduation, Ethan continued his interest and pride in his culinary skills by finding a job in food service.

Ethan was eager to share his grandmother's recipe for apple crumb cake. He enjoyed cooking and baking and appeared more motivated in Food Lab than in any of his other classes. I am unsure which of the sixteen factors of intrinsic motivation was the most important, but many of them applied in his case. He described how his grandmother used to grate the apples by hand and how her knuckles became bruised in the process. Using the food processor eliminated the need for any of the pain. This cake is moist and delicious and is a wonderful dessert for a crowd. It has become one of my favorites.

LITHUANIAN APPLE CRUMB CAKE
Serves 12

INGREDIENTS
1¾ sticks butter, softened

3 eggs. Lightly beaten

4 cups flour

1 cup sugar

2 tsp baking powder

1 tsp vanilla

8-10 firm apples, peeled and shredded or grated

¾ cup sugar/cinnamon/nutmeg mixture (proportions to your taste)

Lemon juice

Vanilla ice cream to serve with cake

DIRECTIONS
Preheat oven to 350 degrees. Grease 11"x16" cookie sheet or 13"x9" baking pan on sides and bottom.

With your hands, combine softened butter, eggs, flour, sugar, baking powder, and vanilla until crumbs form. (This is a sticky, messy job. I took a chance and used the food processor's steel blade to make the crumbs and it worked perfectly.)

Sprinkle half of the crumbs on bottom of greased pan.

Shred apples in food processor using grating disk. If necessary, grate apples by hand.

Toss with cinnamon/sugar mixture and sprinkle with lemon juice.

Place apples on top of dough; then spread remainder of crumbs over top.

Bake for 50-60 minutes until browned and firm. When cool, slice into squares to serve.

This recipe freezes well so you can always have a batch around to serve guests.

And then there was Ani, who had some vague memory of her family's Armenian heritage. She did not know much about that part of her history. When our class took a field trip to an Armenian cultural museum, she was intrigued to learn the deep and broad impact that family members had made in developing the Armenian culture in Watertown, Massachusetts, one of the largest Armenian communities in the world outside of Eastern Europe. Seeing her family name in a few of the exhibits was thrilling and inspired Ani to ask for more information. It also inspired the class to investigate and cook some Armenian recipes. Bringing this experience into the Food Lab, tasting the food, and learning more about the culture brought a living history lesson into Threshold. Observing the exhibits and learning about the controversy over the possibility that genocide had been committed led to many discussions. Seeing some artwork produced by a loyal Armenian, Dr. Kevorkian also contributed to active conversations with many differences of opinion about Kevorkian's philosophy on assisted suicide.

Ani didn't know much about her Armenian heritage but once introduced to the culture in a visit to a museum, she was eager to gain more knowledge. Visiting some of the markets in the ethnic community and preparing and tasting the food brought her heritage to life. Rice pilaf crossed cultures and was recognized and appreciated by other students for its taste and texture.

ARMENIAN RICE PILAF
Serves 4

INGREDIENTS
½ stick (4 tbs) butter
¼ cup minced yellow onions or scallions
½ cup vermicelli pasta crumbled into 1 inch long pieces
1 cup basmati, mahatma, or other long grain white rice
1½ cups prepared chicken broth
½ cup water
(Or, use 2 cups water and 2 chicken bouillon cubes)
1 tsp salt
½ tsp pepper
½ cup pine nuts
½ cup chopped dry apricots

DIRECTIONS
Melt butter in deep covered saucepan. Add minced scallions or onions and sauté until softened.

Add crumbled vermicelli and sauté until golden brown.

Add rice, chicken broth and water, and salt and pepper and mix well.

Bring to boil, then lower heat, cover pot, and simmer for 25 minutes until rice is tender and all liquid is absorbed. Turn off heat and let sit for few minutes. Add apricots and pine nuts to blend together.

Stir pilaf and serve.

For some students, their heritage can be almost downplayed even within the family. Sometimes, the students don't even know much about their personal history. They might have heard hints, but in certain circumstances it was only through food that they learned the secrets.

Anna was aware that her family had come to the United States from Russia. Her mother and other relatives taught her some of their stories through their meals. Perhaps because of religious persecution, the family had to minimize their Jewish roots. It was the recipes that she contributed to our class that provided the best view of her history. Anna helped prepare potato latkes for a Chanukah celebration which offered her an opportunity to illustrate her background in a safe way.

She was also very proud of her delicious Summer Soup. While cooking with her classmates, she was able to share more family stories and information about Russia and the culture of her ancestors with pride and satisfaction as she received compliments on the unique taste.

Anna did not share much about her heritage in conversation. It was obvious from her ease in the kitchen that she had some instruction in traditional Russian cooking. In the late spring, she shared this recipe and began to talk a bit more about some of her family history and the secrets they were forced to keep. Because she was not a verbal communicator, she was much better able to share her knowledge and abilities by doing rather than telling. Even students who claimed to dislike beets gave the sweet and tangy vegetable a second chance. This soup is usually served with brown bread covered with sweet butter.

RUSSIAN SUMMER SOUP
Serves 4-6

INGREDIENTS

2 jars of prepared beet soup (borscht; you can make the soup from scratch, but it is messy and time consuming and the prepared liquid tastes really good, as my mother-in-law agreed)

2 potatoes, scrubbed, peeled, and chopped into bite-sized pieces

2-3 eggs

7-8 radishes

2-3 fresh pickling cucumbers

3-4 scallions, including green leaves

½ lb of cooked meat (bologna is traditional but chicken works), cut into small chunks

Sour cream, to taste

Fresh dill

Salt/pepper to taste

DIRECTIONS:

Boil potatoes in saucepan until soft but not mushy. Remove potatoes to drain. Set aside to cool.

Boil eggs until hard (20 minutes). Set aside to cool. Peel and chop into bite-sized pieces.

Clean, peel, and cut all vegetables into small cubes. Put all chopped ingredients into large bowl and stir together gently, Food should keep chunky texture.

Place 2-3 tablespoons of chopped mixture into soup bowls for serving.

Pour beet soup over mixture in bowl. Place teaspoon of sour cream in each bowl. Sprinkle with chopped fresh dill and salt/pepper to taste.

Pass additional sour cream as desired.

Victor took pride in part of his heritage, but had little opportunity to share and educate others about his Ethiopian ancestry. For his Food Lab assignment, he asked his father for a recipe that they had cooked together. One of the ingredients was particular to Ethiopian cooking and was not used in any other cuisine. I expressed concern that Victor would have trouble finding the particular bread that was an essential component for eating the traditional food. An Ethiopian dinner consists of many small plates of well-spiced meats and vegetables that are served on a large tray. No utensils are used, but instead the special spongy bread is used to pick up bits of the food before placing it on one's plate and then into your mouth. He was proud to say that he had discovered a source of "injera" and would take the responsibility to buy the product and deliver it to class the week that we would prepare his recipe. Victor came through. The recipe was unique and the injera made the meal different from anything that anyone else had cooked and perhaps had ever eaten. Cooking and eating the food together gave Victor a chance to share some memories he had inherited along with the recipe. This recipe provided a great example of "experiential learning" and offered a source of pride for Victor.

For some students from diverse backgrounds, or who are second-generation American citizens, connecting with family heritage can be complicated. Although there is shared pride and history, there is also sometimes some confusion and mixed messages that are passed on. For many, it is only in the food traditions that the clear and pleasant memories are transferred. Victor's father wore traditional Ethiopian dress, and gave the best picture of his culture through the recipes that were passed on. The traditional bread, injera, was essential to the meal. The smile on Victor's face when he took the first bite indicated that he tasted his history.

HAGO'S TIBS-BEEF KIFTO (ETHIOPIAN STYLE)
Serves 4-6

INGREDIENTS
2 tbs vegetable oil
2 tbs butter
1-2 lbs very lean sirloin, cut into bite-sized pieces
1 tsp mixed spices: salt, pepper, garlic powder, cinnamon
1 small red onion, peeled and chopped into bite-sized pieces
1 red pepper, seeded and chopped
1 carrot, peeled and sliced thin
1 clove garlic, minced fine
Juice of 1 lemon
2-4 tsp hot sauce or chili sauce
Salt, pepper, and basil flakes to taste
Injera: Ethiopian bread used to scoop and serve meat. You can find this in some Asian or other international markets.

DIRECTIONS:
Put butter and oil into large skillet. When oil is warm and butter melted, add beef and brown lightly. Remove beef from skillet.

Sauté vegetables in skillet 3-4 minutes. Return meat to skillet.

Sprinkle spices over meat. Cook meat and vegetables together for 3-4 minutes.

Sprinkle lemon juice over all.

Pour chili sauce over top and stir all together. Taste to correct seasoning and add water as necessary. Serve with injera.

All of these examples are just a sample of the many bonding experiences that developed while cooking together. Learning through cooking was so natural and helped students acknowledge and accept their differences and similarities. As an educator, I was amazed at all that I learned and could use as teachable moments from the process of the food preparation and discussion over the meal.

CHAPTER 7

ISLANDS OF COMPETENCE

"Seek out that particular mental attribute which makes you feel most deeply and vitally alive, along with which comes the inner voice which says, 'This is the real me,' and when you have found that attitude, follow it.'
— James Truslow Adams

Dr. Robert Brooks, a faculty member of Harvard Medical School, is one of my heroes. A long time ago, when I heard him speak at a conference describing a theory that he developed after working with children with learning disabilities, I realized that his philosophy matched my own natural instinct. Brooks said, after hearing people of various ages describing what life had been like for them, "While reflecting upon negative comments, I thought, 'Many of these children and adults seem to be drowning in an ocean of self-perceived inadequacy.' " This image remained with Brooks for a few moments, but was soon replaced by another, namely, "If there is an ocean of inadequacy, then there must be islands of competence—areas that have been or have the potential to be sources of pride and accomplishment." Continuing with this metaphor, he said, "I recall thinking with some excitement, we must help children and adults to identify and reinforce these islands, so that at some point they become more dominant than the ocean of inadequacy."

Even before Dr. Brooks published his books describing his theory, I saw these "islands" in the many young adults with whom I have worked. Because I began my career as a vocational rehabilitation counselor, I needed to help the clients discover their essential skills and interests. Most clients' received vocational assessment and testing. I had the chance to review their reports, but it was usually not until I had the opportunity to really get to observe the individuals with whom I worked, and talk to them about their personal histories, that I was able to find the best match and the right job for the client. Even before the recession, when jobs were more plentiful, it was still challenging to put all the pieces together to find jobs for people with disabilities that might develop into positions where both the employer and the new employee could develop mutual long-term satisfaction. Now, with the recession and the dramatically increased rate of unemployment even for people without disabilities, the challenge has exponentially expanded. Helping someone define the elements of his/her values, skills, interests, and training and matching them with an available position is complicated, but essential. Internships are a wonderful way to explore options. For many years, with many different clients, I tried to put the pieces of the puzzle together to guide a client into a job that could offer satisfaction and growth potential. When I transitioned into my new role as the Food Lab instructor, I could sometimes get a vision of the puzzle pieces clicking together to offer a vision of potential career possibilities as I cooked with the students.

Matt's situation demonstrated how this could happen. He really needed to find a new island, after a serious accident left him a different person than he had been before he turned sixteen. Suddenly the lacrosse star headed to an Ivy League university had to start from square one. He had to learn to deal with a hearing loss and other physical complications as well as the learning challenges that traumatic brain injuries can cause. Although when he looked in the mirror, a handsome young man with a warm, supportive family looked back at him, he had to begin to realize that he was not at all the same person that he had been. Matt had to adapt to so many changes in his body while he searched for a new area of competence on which to rebuild his dreams and confidence. He did not enjoy working with children, although they liked getting to know him. Working in an office wasn't a good match for his attributes either, so he needed help broadening his career exploration. Occasionally faculty working with him in the classroom setting found it difficult to communicate with him due to his hearing issues, which made his speech patterns different, and his defiant attitude, which further complicated his learning. Trying to guide him and place him in a meaningful internship where he could maximize his learning and establish a path for future growth was complex.

One of the favorite activities in Food Lab was the end of the semester celebration where the second-year students held a party for the first-year students. The students planned the party, decided which foods would be most interesting and appropriate, shopped for the ingredients, and prepared the finger foods and sweets that worked well at a "mock-tail" party. Although they developed a clear list of responsibilities and defined who was going to do what, at the end of the party, the clean-up crew lost energy and dissipated. Only Matt, a first-year invited guest, stayed behind. I explained that as a guest, he was not expected to finish the work and polish up the kitchen. But he claimed that he loved working in the kitchen. He and I spent a good hour working together. I was amazed and thrilled to see how capable he was in the kitchen. He worked efficiently. There was little evidence of his physical limitations. He talked about his love of food and cooking. He described how much he loved to go fishing and cook and eat seafood. He mentioned how essential it was to keep the kitchen clean as he cooked. Matt said that he particularly liked to go to fancy restaurants with his family to eat really tasty food. There was little evidence of his speech and hearing limitations as we worked together one-on-one. His enthusiasm was contagious and I suddenly had insight into his island.

The vocational faculty at Threshold used all their resources to identify volunteer internship sites in the greater Boston area. The director of Threshold had a broad social circle and was kind enough to stay on the lookout for places where an intern might have a learning opportunity. He asked a good friend, who happened to be the proprietor of one of the best restaurants in the area, if he might consider offering a student with the interest in food service an opportunity to develop some skills in the kitchen. Over the years, Paul was cooperative and offered several Threshold students a chance to see a new world, behind the scenes in an esteemed restaurant. After their year of slicing, chopping, stirring, and observing the mechanics in a restaurant kitchen as an intern, upon graduation several of those people used their training to stay in the food service field and find employment. Since this pattern was our goal, both Paul and the faculty advisor realized that this could be a "win-win" situation for the students whose skills and interests matched the requirements of the field. The Threshold student would gain valuable skills, experience, and perhaps even references in the field, and Paul could give his kitchen staff some assistance with the routine work while doing the service of helping a young adult explore a career possibility.

When I mentioned this opportunity to Matt as a possibility for his second-year internship, he considered it for a minute. He asked if it was a really good restaurant. When I reassured him that it was one of the best in the area, he became excited. He asked good questions about the work and his responsibilities. I explained that he should think about it over the summer and I would begin the discussion with the owner. Suddenly, Matt had a vision of the future that seemed brighter than what he had previously imagined. He did not yet realize what it would take for him to develop the skills, work attitude, competence, and confidence in the food service field, but, at least, he had a glimpse that there might be the potential of an island out there for the new Matt.

Matt's father was equally excited about the possibility, but was cautious about his son's ability to start at the lowest rung of the career ladder. We discussed how we could work together to remind Matt that everyone, with or without a disability, had to get through the "hard knocks," the initiation rituals that a new career, even with the best training, could bring. Throughout the first semester, the warnings that Matt's father offered became evident. Although he claimed to like the work, and enjoyed the people with whom he was working, Matt displayed frustration with the repetitive, less than exciting tasks that both he and the other culinary employees had to accomplish day after day. It took some threats, inducements, and lots of conversations before Matt could accept the reality that he, like everyone else in the field, had to start at the bottom. As he continues to mature and gain more experience and self-knowledge, hopefully he will be able to develop a set of skills that will help him move forward. As Dr. Stanley Ira Greenspan, an Ivy-League trained medical professional who had some learning difficulties, told the *Washington Post* in 1996, discussing his own challenges, "People have an enormous capacity to compensate for any areas of vulnerability." It is one of our goals at Threshold to try to help the students find the areas and the techniques to learn to compensate.

Matt had many things to discover about himself. He did know that he loved to cook, especially seafood. He was rarely as engaged, enthusiastic, and confident as he was when he was the head chef preparing some of his specialties. His island of competence was reflected in his performance in Food Lab.

PASTA WITH CLAM SAUCE
Serves 4

INGREDIENTS
2 6.5-oz cans minced clams, with juice
¼ cup butter
½ cup vegetable or olive oil
½ tsp minced garlic
1 tbs dried parsley (can substitute 3 tbs minced fresh parsley)
Ground black pepper to taste
¼ tsp dried basil
1 16-oz package dried linguini
Grated parmesan cheese, if desired.

DIRECTIONS
Boil water in large pot. When water comes to full boil, sprinkle a dash of salt and oil into pot to prevent sticking. Break pasta up to fit into pot. Stir pasta and cook according to package directions.

While pasta is cooking, combine clams with clam juice, butter, vegetable oil, minced garlic, parsley, basil, and pepper in large saucepan. Place over medium heat and heat to boiling.

When pasta is ready, put into serving bowl. Cover with warm sauce and serve.

Sprinkle with grated parmesan cheese, if desired.

It was important to remind myself that even when a student demonstrated an island of competence, this alone might not always bring the confidence and self-esteem that Dr. Brooks described. Jen came to the Threshold Program planning to major in early childhood education. Both she and her parents felt that she had talent and interest in working with children. They were also pleased with the notion that by completing the two years of training and internship experience that the class provided, Jen could earn the credentials required to become a preschool teacher in the state of Massachusetts. The agency that certified the training required particular coursework and the completion of a precise number of hours in a licensed daycare center supervised by a qualified teacher in order to earn the credentials. Although she enjoyed working with the children most of the time, she was not always able to stay in class long enough to hear the whole lesson nor was she able/willing to finish the written work that demonstrated understanding of the topic. Even with all possible accommodations to fit her learning style, she felt too frustrated to follow the syllabus and do the homework. Therefore, she was always behind in her work and her comprehension of the material. She began to feel less and less comfortable in both the class and the internship. She needed both the internship hours and the academic credits she would earn if she was successful in the class in order to get her certificate. This conundrum developed an ongoing tornado. Jen wasn't going to classes, wasn't completing her assignments, was missing hours at her internship, and was feeling miserable and acting out. The only class that she attended regularly and used as her refuge was the cooking class. After the first few classes, when her unusual skill and comfort level in Food Lab were recognized, Jen revealed that she had completed a year of culinary arts training at a post-high school program for young adults with learning disabilities. She demonstrated well-developed skills with knives and she had a solid understanding of kitchen hygiene and maintenance. She had a good feel for seasoning and solid experience or instinct for making basic ingredients taste better. She was the natural leader in the class because of her expertise and confidence. Here was the one place that she could relax, enjoy, and perform to her highest capacity.

When at the end of the semester, Jen said that she no longer felt she had the patience to work with children; it seemed like a natural progression to give her an opportunity to match her instincts and abilities with a different career direction. When she mentioned that she also had some experience working with seniors, I thought I had discovered her island of competence. I called a particular supervisor, with a great deal of patience and empathy for our population, who directed a day program for elderly patients with mental illness. I asked if she would be willing to take an intern to work in her food service program preparing and serving breakfast and lunch to the program participants. It seemed like a good match. Jen started out very well. She learned to travel to the site easily and became involved with some of the participants. She sent up the sandwiches, and learned to puree food for those members of the program who required that service. She did an excellent job cleaning and sanitizing the cooking and dining areas. She had some difficulty accepting direction from the kitchen manager, but claimed to understand the kitchen hierarchy. And then, suddenly, she developed a few physical ailments, had a few accidents, shared too much personal information with her co-workers, and the tornado developed again, even without the stress of written homework as the trigger point. In this case, not even finding an island was the answer to help someone move forward. It will take more time and professional expertise to help this young lady find the place where she can put her talents, interests, and issues to work.

While some students displayed a level of competence and confidence in the kitchen, and it seemed to represent an island of competence, unless the individual buys into it and believes and wants this island to turn into a direction, neither I nor anyone else can make it happen. For Jen, this recipe displayed her solid skills and interests in cooking. Her pride and satisfaction were evident, but it was not enough to alter her life decisions. The recipe is fast and easy to produce, and the chicken is both sweet and zingy. Adjust the paprika to your taste.

CHICKEN PAPRIKASH

INGREDIENTS
2 tbs olive oil
2 lbs. boneless chicken breasts, trimmed of fat and cartilage and cut into bite-sized pieces
1 small red pepper and 1 small green pepper, trimmed, seeded, and cut into bite-sized pieces
4 generous tbs Hungarian paprika
1 16-oz container of sour cream
1 cup chicken bouillon
1 package thick egg noodles or white rice to serve with chicken

DIRECTIONS:
Warm olive oil in large skillet. Sauté chicken. When chicken is almost fully cooked, with no pink meat showing, add peppers to skillet.

Once peppers are beginning to soften, add paprika to chicken mixture and cook together for 3 minutes. Chicken, pepper, and paprika mixture should form a thick dark blend. Taste the sauce. If it is not dark and tangy, add more paprika.

Stir in bouillon.

Salt and pepper to taste can be added also.

Add sour cream, stir well and let cook together over low heat for 5-10 minutes.

Begin cooking noodles when you add sour cream.

Serve chicken warm over noodles or rice.

Lindsay was an example of a young adult whose ability to function in certain areas defied her tested abilities. Each year, there were students accepted into the program from the waiting list. Reviewing the applications of some of these applicants, they did not seem to be an exact match for the criteria for admission. They were usually short in one area of testing or didn't complete the diagnostic evaluation as expected. Lindsay was a very attractive, composed young lady whose academic scores were all at the very lowest level considered. She wanted to work with children and had a solid base of work experience and references from her background in childcare. She was admitted and worked diligently in all the classes. She tried hard to keep up with the coursework and used the academic support services. She admitted that her primary focus was to get married, make a home, and find a job working with children. Most of the classes were challenging for her, but she demonstrated her affinity for working with children and when she began the cooking class, I recognized that she was fortunate. Her dreams and goals were a good match for her abilities. She was a natural in the kitchen. She enjoyed cooking and had a great understanding of kitchen cleanliness and safety. Her recipes were delicious, simple, and well received by everyone. It was evident that with the support of her future husband and family, she would be able to manage to live independently, certainly in the food domain. Lindsay had her island. She was definitely an example of a chance well taken. It would have been unfortunate if her test scores had been the only means to assess her readiness for the Threshold Program. It would have been a loss all around if she had been denied this experience.

Cooking and kitchen management exemplified Lindsay's island of competence.

CHICKEN MARSALA LINDSAY
Serves 4-6

INGREDIENTS
1½ lbs boneless chicken breasts
¼ cup flour
½ tsp salt
¼ tsp pepper
½ tsp dried basil (can substitute dried rosemary)
3 tbs butter or margarine
2 tbs olive or vegetable oil
4-8 oz fresh mushrooms
½ cup Marsala wine (can use Marsala cooking wine with reduced alcohol content)

Cooked rice or pasta makes a good side dish

DIRECTIONS
Trim boneless chicken of all fat and cartilage. Cut into bite-sized chunks.
Combine flour, salt, and other seasoning in plastic bag.
Heat butter and oil in heavy nonstick skillet over medium heat.
Place cubed chicken pieces in plastic bag with seasoning ingredients and shake well. (Another way to dredge—coat—the chicken would be to put seasoning into shallow bowl and dip chicken pieces into flour mixture.)
Cook coated chicken in butter/oil until lightly browned on all sides and no longer pink.
Add mushrooms to skillet and stir well.
Pour Marsala wine into pan.
Cover pan and simmer over low heat for ten minutes.
Prepare rice or pasta while chicken is cooking.

Mike was a pleasant young man who was usually agreeable and willing to do whatever was asked of him. He never demonstrated much passion for anything other than his girlfriend, until he began his Food Lab class. Suddenly another side of this person became visible. He loved to cook and had a solid base of skills. He enjoyed sharing recipes and hints from his family cooking tradition. He even went on to using his skills and interests in both a volunteer internship in a hospital cafeteria and then a position in a university cafeteria after graduation. This recipe was adapted from Ina Garten's Barefoot Contessa *cookbook. Mike enjoyed eating it so much that he asked his mother to send it on for his contribution to the class.*

LINGUINE WITH SHRIMP SCAMPI (A LA BAREFOOT CONTESSA)
Serves 4-6

INGREDIENTS

1 tbs vegetable oil

1½ lbs linguine (you can use whole wheat variety)

6 tbs unsalted butter

5 tbs olive oil

3 tbs minced garlic (about 6-8 cloves)

2 lbs large shrimp peeled and deveined (shrimp should be at least medium-sized: 26-30 per lb)

Salt and pepper to taste

¾ cup chopped parsley

Grated zest of one lemon

½ cup freshly squeezed lemon juice (from 3-4 lemons, or use frozen concentrate or bottled lemon juice)

¼ tsp dried hot pepper flakes (to taste)

DIRECTIONS:

Place 1 tbs vegetable oil into large pot of water. Set to boil, add salt and when water is rapidly boiling, break linguine into pieces and stir into water. Cook for 7-10 minutes until softened (check package directions) stirring occasionally.

Meanwhile, in another large skillet, melt butter and olive oil together over medium-low heat. Add garlic and sauté for 1 minute.

Add shrimp, salt, and pepper and sauté just until shrimp turn pink, about 5 minutes.

Remove from heat and add parsley, lemon zest, lemon juice, and red pepper flakes. Toss well.

When pasta is ready, drain linguine and put back into pot with shrimp and sauce. Toss all together and serve immediately.

CHAPTER 8

RESPECT FOR DIFFERENCES

Although most of the students enrolled in Threshold have had a living example of the pain and discomfort that feeling different than others can cause, most of them didn't realize how they might have contributed to some form of discrimination themselves. Each student was raised within a particular ethnic, racial, religious, or cultural community and often lacked familiarity with different customs. Even those students who had learned the history of the civil rights movement in America may not have recognized how their upbringings impacted their life. Each family, reflecting their own heritage, culture, and taste, interpreted even the most basic meals in unique ways. Food Lab provided an excellent opportunity to explore and discuss some of their similarities and differences in a non-threatening, productive, and safe way.

Exposing students to kosher traditions was interesting. Most of them had heard of kosher hot dogs or knew that some people couldn't eat certain foods for religious reasons, but it wasn't until the students experienced cooking kosher style or transforming recipes to comply with other traditions that they could fully appreciate the mechanics. A small number of students, who practiced strict kosher principles, could not eat any of the food we prepared in the lab kitchen because the pots, dishes, and utensils, let alone the ingredients with which we cooked, did not comply with their dietary needs. The majority, whose traditions were more liberal, were able to inform the other students about their historic rituals and regulations.

Rebecca came from a strong religious tradition that might have precluded her from participating in many of the activities that were incorporated in the program. When considering how she could maintain her kosher tradition while joining in the Food Lab, she and her family decided, with flexibility, she could continue to observe her dietary restrictions, while preparing and eating some of the food in the lab. She felt pride in giving her classmates some understanding of the basic rules of Kasruth (kosher culinary rules) like the fact that foods containing dairy and/or meat had to be separated in both preparation and eating. She demonstrated the symbols on food packages that indicated what kind of meal, dairy or meat, these foods matched and also indicated that these items conformed to defined rules that allowed them to be eaten by people who followed the kosher practice. She especially enjoyed preparing and eating some of her favorite foods like the spinach quiche or noodles and rice that she grew up with.

Other members of the class began to try to figure out what and how to transform recipes so that Rebecca could share them. Although they knew that grilled cheese sandwiches with bacon and tomatoes were delicious, they began to realize that the bacon had to be eliminated from her portion. Students began to recognize that Rebecca's sandwich even had to be prepared in a different skillet so that hers would have no contact with the bacon.

Rebecca was a very slender person. She came from a well-established religious background. Because she tried to maintain her kosher tradition, it was difficult to know whether she was so slim partly because she had to restrict her eating. Or perhaps her eating tradition was so healthy and nourishing that she didn't gain extra weight from eating too much fast food. She really enjoyed sharing some of the recipes from her family kitchen and her classmate gained insight into changing recipes to fit individual needs.

REMARKABLE EGGPLANT PARMESAN
Serves 8

INGREDIENTS
Sauce:
4 cloves garlic, peeled and minced
2 tbs olive oil
1 28-oz can crushed tomatoes
2 tbs fresh parsley, washed and chopped
Pinch salt and freshly ground pepper
1 bay leaf
Pinch of sugar

Eggplant:
4 eggs beaten
¾-1 cup flour
2 1-lb. eggplants, unpeeled, washed, and sliced into ½ inch round slices
Soybean or canola oil for frying
1 lb. mozzarella cheese, thinly sliced

DIRECTIONS
Sauté garlic in oil. When it starts to turn golden, add the tomatoes with their juice. Break up each tomato. Bring to boil. Add parsley, salt, pepper, sugar, and bay leaf. Let boil for another 2 minutes, and then reduce heat to simmer. Simmer for 45 minutes. Remove bay leaf. Remove from heat and let stand for 5 minutes before pouring over eggplant.
Preheat oven to 350 degrees.

Pour eggs into shallow bowl and beat with whisk. Put flour into another shallow bowl. Use fork to dip eggplant slices into egg, then flour mixture, until lightly coated.

Pour oil into skillet and heat. Fry slices 3 minutes on each side until browned. Drain on paper towel.

Coat baking pan with cooking spray. Put a layer of fried eggplant in pan, then a layer of thinly sliced mozzarella cheese. Then add another layer of eggplant. Repeat layers until there are 3 layers of each. You can add a thin layer of tomato sauce to the eggplant stack before baking, or add the tomato sauce immediately before serving.

Bake for 30 minutes until cheese is golden.

Gabe was experimenting with observing the kosher tradition. He contributed a recipe that proved that it was possible to maintain the rules without sacrificing taste or diversity. Although some of the ingredients sound unusual and foreign, you can find most of them in the Asian aisle of most large supermarkets.

TASTY SZECHUAN SESAME NOODLES
Serves 4

INGREDIENTS
Sauce

2 tbs sesame paste or tahini sauce (you can find this in the supermarket or Asian market)

2 tbs soy sauce

1 tbs hot chili oil (more or less to your taste)

2 tbs sesame oil

½ tbs rice vinegar

1 tsp sugar

1/3 cup hot water

12 asparagus spears

4 scallions

3 bundles soba (buckwheat) noodles OR 1-lb package of linguini

DIRECTIONS
If using tahini, stir tahini until all oil is mixed in. Sesame paste does not usually separate.

Whisk together all sauce ingredients in bowl and set aside.

Fill large soup pot ¾ full with water and set to boil.

While waiting for water to boil, trim asparagus into bite-sized pieces. Discard ends of asparagus. Place trimmed pieces in microwave-safe bowl with ¼ cup water. Cover with plastic wrap and heat in microwave for 3 minutes. Remove from microwave; lift cover carefully (pull wrap off away from face, and use potholder). Drain asparagus and rinse in cold water to keep crisp.

Prepare scallions by trimming off root ends; chop remainder into small pieces.

Cook soba noodles for about 5 minutes. Check package directions for cooking time for linguini. Drain noodles when they reach the right texture, then rinse.

Place noodles in bowl. Stir in sauce, then asparagus and scallions.

Because Bridge Year students had fewer required classes and more work experience, they also had more time in their academic day to cook. We therefore had more opportunity to explore different cuisines and celebrate holidays with feasts, where we cooked together, invited others, and discussed how/why these holidays were celebrated in different homes and different cultures. Our Thanksgiving, Hanukah, and Passover/Easter meals became famous on campus.

There were several simple recipes that represented one particular holiday for people coming from one culture, but was also recognized and appreciated by people from many different backgrounds. When Tal asked to make potato pancakes or latkes to celebrate Hanukah in December, other students were delighted. There was much discussion over the many different recipes, cooking processes, ingredients, and accompaniments. It became a bonding experience because the students recognized similarities in their personal histories that had been unrecognized until that time. Students really bonded over latkes.

POTATO PANCAKES (LATKES)
Makes 20 small pancakes

INGREDIENTS
4 large potatoes, peeled and stored in cold water
1 small onion, peeled
2 eggs
2 tbs matzo meal or flour
½ tsp baking powder
Salt and pepper

DIRECTIONS
There is much disagreement about the perfect way to prepare latkes. Probably every way works fine. The most important thing to remember is to keep the peeled potatoes in cold water so they don't discolor, and to drain the mixture before frying it so that the latkes are not too starchy or soggy.

You may peel the potatoes completely or leave some skin, which has been scrubbed carefully. Some people make latkes substituting sweet potatoes or zucchini for white potatoes, following the same recipe.

Quarter the potatoes and onion. Chop a few pieces of potato and one quarter of the onion together until coarsely chopped. This can be done using a food processor or a hand grater. Place chopped mixture in colander or strainer and press to remove excess liquid.

Add eggs, matzo meal or flour, and seasoning. Mixture should be a thick liquid similar to pancake batter.

Place ½ inch vegetable oil into large griddle or frying pan. Turn heat to high (turn on exhaust fan to prevent smoke detector from buzzing). Test to check temperature of oil by sprinkling with water. When water bubbles, oil is ready.

Scoop about 1/8 cup of batter into hot oil. Fill griddle, leaving some space between pancakes. Fry pancakes until firm and lightly browned on one side, then flip over and fry other side. Pancakes should be brown and edges should be crispy.

Drain latkes on paper towels. You can store the completed pancakes in oven set at 175-200 degrees to keep them warm as you prepare other batches.

Serve latkes with applesauce (see following recipe), sour cream, or sugar depending on family tradition.

This applesauce is multi-seasonal. It crosses traditions also. It is wonderful in the fall, when fresh apples have just been picked. It works well with potato pancakes and other holiday food traditions. Using the microwave is optional: just boiling and hand-mashing apples works well also. The exact texture of the completed sauce is a matter of tradition and personal preference also.

HOMEMADE FRESH APPLESAUCE
Makes 3-4 cups

INGREDIENTS
6-7 medium apples, peeled and cored (you can add cranberries for additional tartness, if desired)

2 tbs water

1 tbs lemon juice

½ cup brown sugar

¼ cup white sugar

NOTE: amount of sugar is personal preference; you can reduce the amount and taste for sweetness

1 tsp cinnamon

½ tsp salt

½ tsp nutmeg (optional)

Fresh lemon juice to sprinkle apples (optional)

DIRECTIONS
Chop the apples coarsely, by hand or in food processor. You should have about 6 cups apples. Sprinkle apples with lemon juice, if desired.

Combine apples with sugars and seasoning and place in 1 to 1½ quart microwave-safe casserole.

Cook apples for 4-6 minutes at medium-high heat. Check for texture: apples should be soft.

Mash apples. Taste and adjust seasoning. Cook a little longer if texture is too firm and flavor has not yet developed.

You can follow the same recipe, adding ½ cup water, and cook on stove top. Bring apples, sugar, water, and spices to boil, then reduce heat and cook slowly for 15-20 minutes. Check for texture, then stir all together and remove from heat.

Refrigerate before serving.

Finding ways to cook and eat together was a graphic example of demonstrating respect for differences. Holding a Seder to celebrate Passover was a perfect way for students to share their traditions and compare similarities and differences through cooking the foods associated with the holiday, decorating the traditional plate, and going through the ritual story as they shared a meal. Students who had not previously attended a Seder learned something about the Passover story and could recognize similar elements in their own religious traditions, for example, that the Last Supper in the Christian Easter holiday tradition may have been a Seder.

Sponge cake is a dessert commonly served at a Passover Seder. Because separating eggs can be challenging, and a Seder meal has many traditional elements, any shortcut is welcome. This cake looks and tastes exactly like the regular one without the extra time or potential for failure.

WHOLE EGG SPONGE CAKE
Serves 8-10

INGREDIENTS
9 eggs

2 cups sugar

6 tablespoons water

2½ teaspoons grated lemon rind (you can also add some orange rind)

1/4 cup lemon juice

3/4 cup matzo cake meal

3/4 cup potato starch

1/2 teaspoon salt

DIRECTIONS
Beat the eggs slightly in electric mixer, then gradually beat in sugar (1/3 cup at a time) and continue beating at high speed, until mixture is thick and yellow.

Add water, lemon rind (and orange rind, if used), and lemon juice. Beat thoroughly. Gradually (to avoid lumps), mix in cake meal and potato starch.

Pour into an ungreased 9-inch tube pan. Bake in a slow oven (325 degrees) for 1¼ hours or until cake springs back when touched lightly.

Invert pan over a narrow-necked bottle and cool thoroughly before removing cake. Be patient because it can take some time for the cake to release from the pan.

Can be served with sliced strawberries or other fruit.

Food allergies offered another opportunity to show understanding and respect for the needs of others. Peanut allergies were complicated because each student with a nut allergy was impacted differently: some students could be safe by simply not eating a recipe that included the allergen, while others could not come in contact with a single piece of food that might have even been touched by a nut. It was essential that the students had a good understanding of their own allergies and were able to communicate with others how they were affected.

For a student like Liz, there could be no peanuts anywhere in the environment. The whole Food Lab community had to research each recipe to ensure that substitutions could always be made for any ingredient that could cause pain and suffering. For students majoring in early childhood education, learning to eliminate nuts or other allergens from the lunch that they brought to their practicum was required because their work environment might be nut-free.

Substituting for one specific ingredient without sacrificing taste and texture was also a valuable lesson in creativity and cooking technique. It was easy to remove nuts while baking brownies or substitute some other product to provide the crunch in salads, but peanut butter kiss cookies had to be eliminated. There were so many other yummy cookies to prepare that the students graciously accommodated. Eliminating cilantro from salsa and other Southwestern recipes was essential if one student had sensitivity to that herb. Finding alternatives to give some zing to the foods was our challenge.

Other food allergies that offered learning options were restrictions on common foods that contained lactose or gluten. Explaining how and why some people develop conditions that prevent them from eating or drinking foods containing certain substances provided basic science education. As someone who has been lactose intolerant since infancy, I find substituting other ingredients for milk, cheese, and ice cream, or taking an antidote natural, but other food sensitivities, like gluten intolerance, proved to be more complicated. First learning to define and understand the gluten process was interesting, and then evaluating when and how to find substitutions was complex. Currently, with awareness increasing in the food community, there are many more gluten-free ingredients, packaged foods, and recipes available. The most essential detail for an individual living with this complicated deficiency is to become well enough informed to protect yourself and explain to others what you need. Celiac disease is defined as a disorder resulting from an immune reaction to gluten, a protein found in wheat and related grains and present in many foods. To protect against damage to the intestines, which can result in an inability to assimilate nutrients, it is essential that those people with celiac disease read every label on every product they consider eating to be sure that there are no elements that might cause them discomfort or potentially dangerous side effects.

Brandon was a young man with many food sensitivities. He was well-informed of his condition and accustomed to altering his diet to meet his needs. He loved to cook and was eager to share some of his favorite recipes. Although this lasagna was different than the common cheese-filled version it proved to be moist and tasty.

GLUTEN FREE, LACTOSE-FREE, AND DELICIOUS LASAGNA
Serves 6-8

INGREDIENTS

1 package rice flour lasagna noodles, available in health food or natural food market

1 lb. ground turkey

1 jar prepared tomato sauce

Italian spices (oregano, garlic)

1 16-oz package lactose-free cheddar cheese

1 8-oz package lactose-free parmesan cheese

DIRECTIONS

Boil 3-4 quarts water in large pot. Insert noodles when water is boiling rapidly. Cook 10 minutes or so (as package directs). Remove to colander to drain.

Grease 9x13-inch baking pan with nonstick spray.

Preheat oven to 350 degrees.

Brown ground turkey in skillet until thoroughly cooked. Drain if needed (turkey is usually very lean so there is little if any grease).

Add tomato sauce and spices and stir together.

Place ½ cup tomato sauce on bottom of prepared pan. Spread around pan to cover. Place one layer of prepared noodles over sauce on bottom of pan.

Sprinkle cheddar cheese over noodles.

Spread another layer of meat sauce over cheese.

Sprinkle with parmesan cheese.

Continue layering noodles, meat sauce, parmesan, and cheddar cheese.

End layers with meat layer, reserving ½ cup cheddar and parmesan cheese.

Cover pan with aluminum foil.

Place lasagna into oven and cook 30 minutes.

Remove foil, sprinkle with cheeses and return to oven until cheeses melt.

Remove from oven and let set for few minutes before serving.

Most often, the students were willing to embrace the adventure of learning to live and eat with substitutions if they were well informed of how and why one had to follow the procedure. Someone who does not carry his or her own identification, both literally and figuratively, could be in an uncomfortable position. Here is an example where it is imperative that a young person needs to "come out" in society with the knowledge to self-disclose and to explain ways to insure their well-being. It is also important that the individual develop the pride, self-confidence, and self-preservation skills to be able to take ownership of their needs. Sometimes, as with celiac disorder, this requires vigilance and communication skills with every meal eaten outside of his/her own home.

Kristen gave us another opportunity to learn to respect and negotiate differences. Because she was legally blind, she taught the other students some of the techniques she used to manage in the seeing world. She was able to demonstrate how to maintain sanitary countertops by following a grid pattern. She was able to chop foods by lining them up in a certain way, and she demonstrated how to store ingredients. Her positive attitude was another valuable tool that she shared with others. It was a constant reminder that each person had to deal with his/her own limitations, and how one learned to confront challenges made all the difference. She recognized her limitations and usually tried to compensate.

She also demonstrated that food preferences did not always follow as systematic a practice as organizing the refrigerator. I felt compelled to try to help those students who came to class with a very well-defined range of food preferences to try to expand their taste buds by trying a wider array of foods. Kristen, one of these students, had a narrow range of foods that she considered acceptable; she refused to eat most vegetables or fruit; she did not like fish, and she was not a big fan of meat or chicken. However, she loved her father's recipe for clam chowder although it was chock full of some ingredients she wouldn't try in other recipes. Reminding her that this soup included fish and many vegetables forced her with great reluctance to consider that maybe things that she had placed on her "unacceptable" list might move to the "give it a chance" category. She learned the value of being a bit more flexible and trying something new. Reminding her and her peers using the "clam chowder" metaphor sometimes worked when she or others were being stubborn about trying something different in their lives.

Although Kristen had a serious visual impairment, some balance issues, and other health considerations, and hated fish and vegetables, this recipe was one of her favorites because it reminded her of her beloved father. She enjoyed cooking this with him and demonstrated the value of all the occupational therapy she had incorporated in the way in which she managed to function in the kitchen. This clam chowder tastes and smells very authentic and is quick and easy to prepare.

CREAMY CLAM CHOWDER
Serves 4-5

INGREDIENTS
4 slices of bacon, diced
1½ cups chopped onions
1½ teaspoons salt
½ tsp ground black pepper
1 tsp dried oregano
2 tsp dried parsley flakes
1½ cups water
4 cups potatoes, scrubbed, peeled, and diced (place potatoes in water to keep from browning)
2 cups half and half
2 tbs butter
2 10-oz cans minced clams (drained, juice reserved)
Soup or oyster crackers for serving

DIRECTIONS:
Place bacon in large stock pot over medium-high heat. Cook until bacon is almost crisp. Add onions and cook together for 5 minutes. Add spices and stir all together.

Stir in water and potatoes. Bring to boil, then reduce heat to medium and cook uncovered for 15 minutes, or until potatoes are fork tender. Do not let them cook until they are mushy.

Pour in half and half, and then add butter.

Stir in drained clams and ½ of the clam liquid.

Cook for 3 more minutes on medium heat until heated though. Do not allow to come to boil.

Serve at once with crackers.

Davina, an Israeli citizen, offered another opportunity to engage with another culture. The idea that someone had left her native country and separated herself from immediate family and friends was surprising to some of the more local contingent. When long weekends or short breaks arrived, she had to visit with a friend or find ways to keep safe and involved on her own. She was not familiar with American traditions like the Fourth of July 4 celebration but was able to share stories about hostilities in the Middle East including learning to sleep during an air raid. So many things, including the snacks and foods that American children grew up with, were different for her which shocked some of the students. Her contributions to the food selections were interesting and provided opportunity for discussions about how and why food traditions develop. Learning about food and culture based on the environment and religious, socioeconomic, and cultural traditions was an important lesson. Her recipe contributions provided constant opportunity for discussions about how and why food traditions develop and how food culture connects with the environment and religious, socioeconomic, and cultural traditions. Seeing how similar traditions existed across cultural lines in the Middle East provided a window into current events. Accepting Davina and getting to know about her world offered a living lesson in cross-cultural education. There was no more visible means of exploring differences and identifying potential bonds between people than cooking, hearing stories, and sharing foods.

This salad recipe was shared by two students, in different years, both reflecting their affection for Israel. One student was a native Israeli who had spent much of her life in the UK and USA, and rarely shared much of her heritage other than in her eating habits and cooking traditions. The other student loved to travel and remember his trips by the foods that he enjoyed while visiting other places. The key to this recipe was the precise chopping of the vegetables. Ingredients can be pre-chopped but dressing should not go on salad until just before serving.

INCREDIBLE CHOPPED ISRAELI SALAD
Serves 4

INGREDIENTS
6 cucumbers
4 Roma or plum tomatoes
1 red pepper
5 green onions
3-4 cloves garlic
1 cup fresh parsley
½ cup fresh mint leaves
½ cup olive oil
2 tbs fresh lemon juice
1 tbs salt
1 tbs ground black pepper (to taste)

DIRECTIONS
Wash all vegetables well.
Cucumbers can be peeled, or left unpeeled. Slice cucumbers lengthwise and remove seeds before dicing into small sections.
Slice, seed, and dice tomatoes and pepper.
Chop green onions. Mince garlic.
Coarsely chop parsley and mint.
Mix all vegetables together in large bowl. (This can be done ahead and reserved until right before serving time)
Drizzle olive oil and lemon juice over vegetables and toss to coat.
Season with salt and pepper and serve immediately.

Rebecca really wanted to share another of her favorite recipes. It complied with her tradition but it was also an example of a comfort food that should be in everyone's recipe collection. When the weather is terrible, you don't feel so good, or you are missing family and friends, going into the pantry and pulling out these basic ingredients can provide a quick, simple meal additive or snack that will warm and fill your tummy.

ANYTIME NOODLES AND RICE
Serves 4

INGREDIENTS
3 cups water
Olive oil
2 cups fine egg noodles
1 envelope dried onion soup mix
1 cup instant white rice

DIRECTIONS:
Place three cups of water into saucepan or teapot. Turn heat to high and get water to active boil.

Cover bottom of large skillet with olive oil. Reduce heat to low. Add noodles and stir around bottom of pan to coat noodles. Sauté noodles until golden brown. Add instant rice and onion soup mix to skillet. Pour boiling water over top and stir to combine.

Simmer all together for 10 minutes, stirring occasionally.

Cover and cook for 10 more minutes.

Cook, checking pan, until all water is absorbed and noodles and rice are soft and ready to eat.

Evan was an international student. Although his primary language was English, his learning challenges made it difficult for him to communicate verbally. Because he was so quiet it was difficult to know if he was interested or involved in any activity. He enjoyed eating and would participate in the cooking and clean-up process in Food Lab. When he submitted his recipe, the complexity of flavors and ingredients was surprising. The taste delighted everyone. He demonstrated an island without using words.

LUSCIOUS LINGUINI
Serves 4

INGREDIENTS
2 cloves garlic
½ lb fresh asparagus
5 oz baby arugula leaves
1/3 lb bacon-strips cut in half
1 16-oz package dried linguini
1/3 cup olive oil
¼ cup fresh lemon juice
Grated parmesan cheese to serve

DIRECTIONS
Peel and slice garlic into thin slices.
Wash, trim, and cut asparagus into ½-inch pieces.
Rinse arugula leaves.
Cook bacon in large skillet over medium heat until browned and crisp. Keep stirring bacon with wooden spoon or spatula so that it doesn't burn. Remove from heat when well cooked and place on paper towels to drain. Chop into small pieces.
Bring large pot of water to boil. Sprinkle salt into water. When water is boiling, break linguini noodles into smaller segments and drop into water. Stir occasionally. Cook for 8-10 minutes or according to package directions. Taste noodles to see if proper texture for your taste. Drain and set aside.
Pour olive oil into skillet. Add garlic and asparagus pieces. Sauté, stirring for 1-2 minutes until just softened.

Add drained pasta to skillet. Turn off heat. Add arugula, lemon juice, and bacon to pan. Stir all together.

Sprinkle with parmesan cheese to serve.

CHAPTER 9

LEARNED HELPLESSNESS

"If we did all the things that we are capable of doing,
we would literally astound ourselves."
                                        —Thomas Edison

Colin came to Threshold with a diagnosis of learning disabilities combined with the uncommon Apert's syndrome. Fused fingers, toes, and altered facial structure characterize this genetic disorder. His physical limitations did not impact his performance as much as his other behavior mannerisms. Although Colin had a tough first year adjusting to the expectations at Threshold, he did comply with one summer assignment in his own fashion. Each summer, I sent a letter to all second-year students asking them to submit recipes that they would like to learn to cook. I told them that they could use any resources—cookbooks, magazines, Internet, favorite family recipes. I even suggested if they loved a particular meal at a restaurant, they could ask the chef for the recipe. Throughout the summer, I received many replies, questions, and ideas about the kinds of foods the students most enjoyed eating. Some recipes came with some comments claiming that he/she was unsure we would be able to make the meal exactly like the recipe, but they wanted to try. I always responded by telling them that those suggestions were exactly what I was looking for. We would experiment together to discover ways to reproduce what they wanted to learn to cook. My goal was to de-mystify cooking and teach them ways they could accomplish eating what they liked without too much time or effort. In Colin's case, his mother sent a recipe for pasta and meat sauce. In a short paragraph she said that she took a box of spaghetti, a jar of prepared meat sauce, and some ready cooked meatballs and put them together for his favorite meal. This gave me a hint that he did not come with a background that included cooking as a favored family activity and tradition.

For the first few weeks of class, Colin sat at the back of the kitchen. He did not volunteer to participate in any of the activities and had to be urged to do even elementary tasks like unloading the dishwasher. He did not take initiative to complete any task, nor was he eager to even put the cutlery, dishes, or glasses away independently; and had to be coached through each step. Although it was a well-defined class rule that each student had to taste one little bite of all the meals we prepared (unless there was some dietary restriction), Colin refused to taste even his token bite, claiming that he wanted to save his appetite for dinner in the dining hall. As we all know, college food in typical dining halls does not offer such a gourmet selection, so that probably wasn't the real draw. Most likely, he was resistant to try what we prepared in the lab. I wondered whether his physical limitations prevented him from comfortably assuming some of the kitchen tasks, so I planned methods to accommodate his limitations. Knowing that pasta and tomato-based sauce was a particular favorite of his, one week when the head chef was preparing stuffed pasta shells, I was able to convince Colin to take the requested one little bite. Although he continued to refuse to assist with the preparation and to hide in his corner, he did sit at the table with his classmates and try the food. After his first bite, he swallowed, smiled, and asked for a little more. When the food was finished, Colin even carried his own plate over to the sink. He needed assistance rinsing his dish before he put it into the dishwasher, and although he didn't offer to help anyone carry any other utensils, he did agree to sponge off the dining table with a little direction. This was a huge step forward. Maybe the old adage "The way to a man's heart is through his stomach" was valid in this situation. Several weeks later, with some gradual and occasional slight loosening of his self-imposed cocoon, he arrived in class to discover that only he and one other student would be responsible for cooking pasta with sautéed vegetables that day.

It would be impossible to ascertain exactly what occurred that moment in time, whether it was the food, his classmate, a very gentle, non-confrontational and supportive young man, or the position of the moon in its planetary movement, but Colin came into the class and asked what he could do. When given his choice of options, he chose to make the pasta. He read the directions carefully, but claimed he didn't know how to boil water. I offered to fill the pan with water, not knowing if he could carry the pot from the sink to the cook top. With instructions, he lit the burners, but wasn't sure what boiling meant. His classmate described how he would know when the water was ready. While we waited for the water to heat up, his classmate worked on preparing the vegetables. Colin asked if he could peel and chop garlic. I was concerned that he wouldn't be able to do it, but once shown; he smashed the cloves of garlic, removed the fine peel, and began to coarsely chop the cloves. When the water started to bubble, he broke the pasta into pieces and put them into the pot. He used a wooden spoon to stir the pasta. He asked good questions about how he would know when the pasta would be ready. As the pasta cooked, the young men worked together to prepare the other ingredients, set the table, and get ready to eat the meal that Colin had really cooked. I was a little anxious when it was time to drain the pasta. Colin wanted to carry it over to the sink to pour it into the colander. Although I was concerned, I realized that it would reinforce the exact behavior that I was trying to reduce if I didn't give him the chance to try something new and challenging. With great trepidation, I made sure the path to the sink was clear and the strainer was in exactly the right position. Colin accomplished this task perfectly also. We combined the pasta, chopped garlic, sautéed vegetables, and spices and sat down to sample our work; Colin took a generous portion, gobbled it, and asked for more. We chatted together, he ate every bite, and he participated actively in the clean-up process.

This class happened close to the end of the semester. Although it would be nice to report a magical transformation, there was not a total turn-around. After that week, Colin came to Food Lab not yet brimming with confidence and energy, but definitely not retreating back into his corner. From that class on, he did participate more, cooperated more, helped with the food preparation and clean-up, and even tasted some of the other food selections. Was there a direct cause and effect relationship between that one week with all the forces aligned and the change in Colin's behavior, or was it more the gradual progression throughout the semester that just became more evident that one week? More significantly, would there be a way to encourage the growth not only in this class, but also in all the facets of his campus experience? And maybe even carry over to his life after college? This will take time to tell.

Martin Seligman (1942-) developed the concept of learned helplessness in the 1960s and 1970s at the University of Pennsylvania. He found that animals receiving electric shocks that they had no ability to prevent or avoid were unable to act in subsequent situations where avoidance or escape was possible. Extending the ramifications of these findings to humans, Seligman and his colleagues found that human motivation to initiate responses is also undermined by a lack of control over one's surroundings. Further research has shown that learned helplessness disrupts normal development and learning and can lead to emotional disturbances, especially depression.

Learned helplessness in humans can begin very early in life if infants see no correlation between actions and their outcome. Institutionalized infants, as well as those suffering from maternal deprivation or inadequate mothering, are especially at risk for learned helplessness due to the lack of adult responses to their actions. It is also possible for mothers who feel helpless to pass this quality on to their children. Learned helplessness in children, as in adults, can lead to anxiety or depression, and it can be especially damaging very early in life, for the sense of mastery over one's environment is an important foundation for future emotional development. Learned helplessness can also hamper education: a child who fails repeatedly in school will eventually stop trying, convinced that there is nothing he or she can do to succeed.

There have been times at Threshold when we recognize that some of the habits, learning styles, and methods of interaction with the faculty and even with other students might have resulted from facets of learned helplessness. We also have examples of students who, whether through decisions made by their family or through their own will, demonstrate the way to combat this tendency. Charlie had physical complications as well as learning challenges, but his positive attitude and determination allowed him to accomplish many things over and beyond expectations.

Charlie was a tall, gangly young man who had physical complications. He had learned compensatory strategies that allowed him to do almost everything. Although one wanted to offer assistance, he would suggest that he try something by himself. He promised to ask for help when he needed it. It was rare that someone had to lend a hand. Although Sloppy Joes tend to be rather uncomplicated, this recipe with a secret had a depth of flavor that made it special.

SLOPPY JOES WITH A SECRET
Serves 6

INGREDIENTS
1 yellow onion
1½ lb ground beef (or ground turkey)
1 cup ketchup
2 tbs unsweetened cocoa powder
1½ tbs yellow mustard
2½ tsp chili powder
1½ tsp black pepper
1½ tsp salt
6 whole wheat rolls to serve

DIRECTIONS
Peel onion, dice into small pieces.
Brown meat in large, deep skillet over medium heat. Put onion pieces in skillet to soften while meat is cooking.
Once meat is browned and onion is soft, stir in ketchup, cocoa, mustard, chili powder, black pepper, and salt.
Heat over medium heat for 15 minutes, stirring occasionally.
Spoon meat mixture over rolls to serve.

Neal Wrightson (2009) director of Children's Community School, a school for special needs students in Van Nuys, California said (in the book *Cowboy & Will*) how important it was "to trust our children to believe they know where they are going and where they need to be. And our job as parents, and the school staff as educators, was to step back and lend a hand, but not direct or peek over their shoulders, constantly making suggestions."

At Threshold, we often see parents, with the best of intentions, who create barriers to learning in their children by not trusting. To protect the children from failure, to ease their path, or to resolve their own feelings of frustration, they may inadvertently have a negative impact on the son's/daughter's ability to learn. As I mentioned, I needed to control my own tendency to step in and do for my son, rather than step back and lend a hand when he asked for it.

Blair had several challenges. In addition to his learning disabilities, he had a family that loved him so much that they gave him everything he could ever want, sometimes even before he knew that he wanted it. He did not complete his summer assignment of sending a recipe. He offered many excuses, for both this lapse and for many other incidents when he neglected to follow through with expectations. He usually began a conversation discussing these issues by saying, "my mother told me," or "my mother did that for me." Although he was fortunate to have an extremely supportive mother, there were many occasions when Blair became paralyzed by his lack of experience in exploring and trying to develop new skills. One summer, he was encouraged to enroll in a class to expand his skills in working with knives, but this experience was not followed by offering him opportunities to practice using the skills for practical purposes like cutting fruits or vegetables. He had a dramatic selection of Japanese swords, and a vast array of electronic equipment, but he did not feel comfortable using a knife to chop an onion or using a computer to type an assignment. Throughout the semester, Blair, with encouragement and close support, did become somewhat more comfortable chopping ingredients, but he never became confident enough to take the responsibility to complete a task on his own, using only his own resources. He tried to delete the expressions he used frequently about his mother having primary responsibility for his actions, but he never, throughout the entire year, completed his primary assignment to find his own recipe to share with his classmates and practice taking leadership in preparing food. Blair did continue to demonstrate his interest in food by taking and succeeding at a job in food service after graduation, preparing food on a grill, assisting customers, and operating the cash register with the guidance and support from a very considerate and cooperative female manager.

Jessica was another example of a young person being held back by the many fears she had developed in taking steps toward independence in the kitchen. She was not at all comfortable using knives or using the stove or oven. She was traumatized by sautéing food in a skillet and needed hand-over-hand instruction to take any responsibility. In the course of the first semester, with encouragement and hand-over-hand direction, she began to try to turn the stove on, or stir something in a hot pot, or even chop a vegetable using a sharp knife and a cutting board. By the end of the semester, with clear directions and support, she was proud to prepare one of her favorite recipes in class. Given additional time and practice, Jessica demonstrated the potential to take care of her basic needs for food and sustenance. She made good progress breaking through the bonds of the learned helplessness that had crippled her.

Every year, and in every class, students wanted to make "mac and cheese". Although there were slight variations in the exact procedure, and the trimmings that were selected, this was always a standard choice. As the supreme comfort food, it was also a good example of the way to make easy tasty recipes "outside the box". Having patience to prepare the cheese sauce is the secret key. It is essential to wait until the milk/flour mixture thickens before adding the cheese.

GOLDEN BAKED MACARONI AND CHEESE
Serves 6

INGREDIENTS:
8 oz dried macaroni
¼ cup butter (4 tbs)
¼ cup flour
2 cups milk
½ tsp salt
¼ tsp pepper
2 cups grated cheddar cheese (can use packaged or grate it yourself), divided into 2 1-cup portions to be used at different times in cooking process
Bread crumbs to sprinkle
Additional spices and flavors can be added: some people like to sprinkle paprika into mix for a little spice and others add Worcestershire sauce

DIRECTIONS:
Preheat oven to 375 degrees.
Spray 8" x 8" or larger baking pan with cooking spray.
Cook macaroni according to package directions. Make sure water is boiling before placing macaroni noodles into pot. Once cooked, drain macaroni well before adding cheese sauce
While macaroni is cooking, prepare sauce.
Melt butter in large saucepan. Stir in flour, and then gradually add milk, stirring constantly to prevent lumps from forming. Add seasoning. Cook slowly over medium heat until sauce thickens. Add 1 cup grated cheese and stir together until cheese melts.

When macaroni is cooked and drained, immediately mix into cheese sauce and combine by stirring well.

Put whole mixture into prepared baking dish. Sprinkle top with bread crumbs and the other 1 cup cheese. Bake in preheated oven for 15 minutes.

If desired, you can remove macaroni from oven and place under broiler for 2-3 minutes until top is brown and bubbly.

Perry presented a different set of challenges. As the son of a trained chef and cooking instructor, his background included learning about fine food. He traveled around the world sampling different cuisines and culinary techniques with his family. He understood the value of using seasoning to develop different flavors and was always willing to help other students spice up their recipes. He was proud of his father's skills and was thrilled when his father joined our class as a guest chef. His father helped the students prepare an outstanding array of recipes including some using one of Perry's favorite ingredients, artichokes.

Perry, Perrin Long's son, loved artichokes. He thought it would be fun for his father to teach a whole class focusing on artichokes. We developed comfort and respect for this prickly vegetable. Making Hollandaise sauce became less complicated once we understood the techniques. Nothing can replace the pleasure of dipping a fresh boiled artichoke leaf in melted lemon butter and Hollandaise sauce, but this esteemed chef shared one of his secrets: prepared, canned artichokes substitute perfectly well for many recipes.

ARTICHOKE DIP

INGREDIENTS
1 cup mayonnaise
1 cup sour cream
¾ cup grated parmesan cheese
2 jars artichoke hearts, drained

DIRECTIONS
Grease or spray with baking spray a 9"x 13" baking pan.
Preheat oven to 350 degrees.
Combine all ingredients in mixing bowl.
Bake for 20 minutes. Serve with crackers or sliced raw vegetables.

HOLLANDAISE SAUCE

INGREDIENTS
2 egg yolks
Juice of ½ lemon
1 stick butter
NOTE: This takes patience and confidence. If you do not have a double boiler, you can use any two saucepans, when one can set comfortably inside the other.

DIRECTIONS
Place all ingredients in top of double boiler. Set water in bottom pan to simmering (water is bubbling but not boiling). Stir ingredients continuously. As ingredients heat up, butter will melt and mixture will be thin. But then, as it warms more, the mixture will begin to thicken. DON'T STOP STIRRING. When mixture is thickened, remove from heat and keep in warm place until ready to use or serve.

We were fortunate to have Perrin Long, a professional chef and educator, make a guest appearance in another class of eight students. Within two hours, the class under his guidance produced four soups from start to finish. It was a remarkable experience in both taste and technique. Everyone learned the value of prep work in getting materials organized and the foods chopped and ready before starting to cook. This recipe proved to be one of their favorites.

FRENCH ONION SOUP
Serves 4

INGREDIENTS
1 tbs butter
1 tbs olive oil
3 medium onions, peeled and sliced into thin rings
Pinch of dried thyme
4 tbs sherry or red wine (cooking wine is a fine substitute)
4 cups of beef broth (store brand is OK)
Salt and pepper to taste
4 croutons (thin slices of French or Italian bread brushed with olive oil and toasted in oven until browned and firm)
8 slices Swiss cheese (sliced into thin strips)

NOTE: You will need 4 ovenproof crocks or small soup bowls to serve this properly)

DIRECTIONS:
Heat butter and oil in large soup pot over medium low heat until butter is melted. Add onions and stir to coat with oil.

Cook the onions over medium heat, stirring occasionally so they soften, but don't burn.

Once onions are tender, add thyme and sherry or wine. Turn heat up and stir until sherry has evaporated.

Add beef broth, bring to boil and simmer, partially covered, for 20 minutes.

Season with salt and pepper.

Place 4 ovenproof bowls or crocks on baking sheet and fill each with hot soup.

Place slice of bread (crouton) on top of soup. Cover with 2 slices of cheese. Place crocks in oven or under broiler until cheese on each is melted and is hot and bubbly.

Serve immediately

Even with his comfort level eating and preparing fine food, Perry was reluctant to submit a recipe of his own. He wanted to have the experience of being head chef, so he finally sent a recipe for French bread pizza, where he covered sliced bread with tomato sauce, sprinkled mozzarella cheese over the bread, and baked it. It will remain a mystery why he found it so difficult to use his well-developed food knowledge and sophistication to select a recipe and gain pride in his own mastery of basic cooking skills. Perhaps perceived learned helplessness played a part; Perry might have felt fearful that he was not yet ready to complete a meal up to his father's level and he might have felt a loss of control over the process. In this situation, the helplessness might not have come from the family holding him back, but more from his own anxiety about comparing his own level of skill and experience to what he witnessed in his family. There was also a possibility that his fear of expressing himself in writing, and his reluctance to use adaptive technology, might have held him back from delivering written work. He will need to continue to work on setting and reaching reasonable expectations. His family will probably reinforce his performance at his level and help him grow.

Perry came from a tradition of eating well, having a chef and cooking teacher for a father and traveling around the world with his family. He had tasted and enjoyed many new flavors and was knowledgeable about seasoning and spices. However, he had little confidence in himself and was not ready to take the leap to try to overcome some fears. This anxiety prevented him from using all his skills and may hold him back from achieving to his full potential. This recipe is an old stand-by that everyone enjoyed. Each person can turn it into their own specialty by adding extra goodies (spinach, mushrooms, olives, etc.).

FRENCH BREAD PIZZA
4 small pizzas

INGREDIENTS
1 loaf of French bread
2 tbs. olive oil
1 jar of prepared pizza sauce or any other pasta sauce
32 slices pepperoni (or whatever topping you prefer)
2 cups grated cheese (mozzarella or any combination of Italian cheeses
Optional seasoning: oregano, garlic, basil etc

DIRECTIONS
Slice bread in half lengthwise and then again to make 4 narrow slices.

Brush each piece with olive oil and toast in oven or toaster oven until light brown.

Top each slice with ¼ cup tomato sauce. Spread sauce over bread evenly.

Add cheese and any other ingredients.

Bake at 375 degrees for 10-12 minutes.

In Alana's case, her family did not seem to understand the value of encouraging their child to try and reach for more independence. Perhaps because they had not had the opportunity to see her perform at her peak, or because they were so fearful that she could not compete, they tended to hold her back. They discouraged, rather than encouraged, her attempts to take steps forward. With that history, Alana was so fearful she might fail that she tended to be reluctant to take chances, even with support. With a great deal of encouragement, she finally decided to share a family recipe that she fondly remembered cooking with her grandmother. Seeing her take charge of the cooking process and teaching everyone else in the class, including the instructor, how to prepare something unique was dramatic. Although she usually sought assistance and/or confirmation with every step in most other circumstances, claiming that she was unsure that she could do something, she demonstrated much more confidence in the cooking realm. She was eager to take her turn as head chef. She glowed as she showed us how to chop garlic, smash tomatoes, and scramble eggs, and prepare the special toast that accompanied her meal. I don't think I ever saw her as cheerful and proud as when she shared the finished product with the class. Sicilian eggs, a la her Italian grandma, were a great success. It was helpful, after this event, to remind her of her competence and confidence whenever she began to repeat her mantra "I don't know if I can do it". She almost always giggled and tried whatever the challenge was with a bit more optimism than she had previously demonstrated. She made a good attempt to overcome her learned helplessness, at least in cooking class, where she recognized her island of competence. Unfortunately, after her graduation, her mother decided that she was not ready to move on to living independently. Hopefully, Alana would be given the opportunity to demonstrate her competence and growing confidence when she went back home.

Because Alana prefaced everything she did with a comment about being unsure that she could accomplish any task, even starting this unusual recipe was a leap for her. Because most often she did not receive encouragement to try to find her own way, she knew that she needed to find some way to fight the helplessness that she felt. Watching her take steps to prepare this recipe, one could almost feel her beloved grandmother's guidance. She taught us the key to success in this recipe was having the patience to stir constantly and wait for it to all come together into a dense, thick mixture. Seeing her pleasure taking a taste of the sweet and tangy combination, confirming that it was exactly the same as she remembered, was worth everything. The combination of breakfast ingredients with spices makes this dish an interesting addition to brunch, lunch, or early supper menus. The experience as head chef offered Alana an opportunity to prove she could do something independently.

GRANDMA'S SICILIAN TOMATOES AND EGGS
Serves 4-6

INGREDIENTS
2 cloves fresh garlic, peeled, chopped, and set aside
¼ cup olive oil
Pinch of salt
2-3 8-oz cans of tomato sauce
10 eggs, beaten
½ cup Pecorino Romano cheese
Firm Italian bread, toasted, buttered, and sprinkled with garlic salt, tastes good with eggs

DIRECTIONS:
Sauté chopped garlic with salt in olive oil in saucepan until soft but not brown.

Add tomato sauce and simmer for 10 minutes over low heat until sauce starts to thicken.

Add beaten eggs to tomato sauce by scrambling them and keeping them constantly moving while cooking over medium heat. Cook until eggs are firm and well cooked.

Sprinkle cheese over top and serve warm with garlic toast.

Sasha demonstrated another set of obstacles. She came to Cambridge from San Francisco, California. She and her mother shared a very close, loving relationship that bordered on co-dependency. They spoke several times each day and it was difficult for Sasha to make any decisions without her mother's input. Although Sasha had never attempted to cook independently, she did enjoy eating and was eager to try to produce some of her favorite recipes. Cooking in class was one activity where she had to reduce her mother's involvement. As head chef, Sasha alone had to take responsibility and leadership. She was nervous at first, but with assistance, she proudly produced one of her quiches. She and her friends gobbled it down and she had one of her first really independent achievements.

Sasha enjoyed eating, cooking, and entertaining. However, she needed to prove to herself that she could do it. She had to battle some elements of learned helplessness. When the salmon quiche came out of the oven, looking, smelling and tasting exactly as she remembered, it reinforced her potential to take the steps to independence. This recipe for basic quiche can be adapted by slightly altering the filling to meet many needs. It works for brunch, lunch, or light dinner. Salmon quiche is awesome: substitute drained canned salmon for ham or bacon.

QUICKIE QUICHE

Makes 2 quiches, enough to serve 10. Can use only one pie shell and reduce ingredients by half to serve 4-5

INGREDIENTS

2 frozen pie shells (removed from freezer for 10 minutes)

1 8-oz package frozen spinach

½ onion

5 oz mushrooms (1 cup sliced)

2 tbs butter

2 eggs, well beaten

1½ cups plain yogurt (nonfat works well)

1 cup milk (whole milk is best, but you can use slightly less nonfat or low fat milk)

Dash salt, pepper, paprika

1 cup chopped ham or cooked bacon

2 cups shredded cheese: cheddar or Swiss works well

DIRECTIONS:

Preheat oven to 400 degrees (or follow crust baking instructions on pie shells).

Set frozen pie shells on cookie sheet.

Defrost frozen spinach in microwave. Drain excess water. Spread evenly on bottom of pie shell.

Prepare onions and mushrooms by washing, peeling, and cutting into thin rings or thin slices.

Sauté mushrooms and onions in skillet in butter. Vegetables should be tender but not over-cooked. Spread vegetables in pie pan.

Combine eggs, yogurt, milk, salt, and pepper by whisking together. Mixture should be well mixed and have consistency of thick milk.

Sprinkle quiche with paprika.

Add ham or bacon (or salmon, etc.) if desired.

Bake in 400 degree oven for at least 45 minutes. Place fork in middle of pie to see that mixture is set firm and not runny. You may need to cook extra 5-15 minutes to reach desired texture. Top should be light brown before removing from oven.

Let quiche set for few minutes before slicing.

CHAPTER 10

PERSONALITY FACTORS AND PERFORMANCE IN THE KITCHEN

Certain factors of individual personality styles impacted directly on the student's ability to perform in the Threshold Program. Although these factors may have had some negative impact in some classes, there were times when in the kitchen environment, the very same modus operandi, which didn't help them accomplish their goals elsewhere, worked. Conversely, there were other students whose behaviors/personal styles were not giving them the best results learning anywhere in the program. For some, even the more relaxed, less demanding class, with the slower pace and the direct reward, did not give those few students the ideal learning opportunity. For some students, the idea that they could not find an environment that offered them a place to use the abilities they did have raised questions about personal issues that most likely would set barriers as they attempted to move on in their lives. For these students getting assistance dealing with some of the issues was essential. Their performance in this class only demonstrated one more red flag.

"Happy Harry" was a young man with a very upbeat, positive personality. He was a cheerful person with an optimistic outlook. He could become very silly when he looked for attention. Although he was well liked by his peers and teachers, he needed to learn when and where he could use his immature, goofy style. Because he planned to work with children as a short-term career goal, with long range dreams to use his passion for fire-fighting, he needed to learn to temper his dancing, singing, and laughing so that he could focus on the tasks that needed to be accomplished. He enjoyed cooking and had role models in his parents and siblings, so he understood that while he was putting a recipe together and preparing a meal, he needed to concentrate. The hands-on nature of the tasks taught him to set aside his frivolous behavior in order to complete the task in a safe and orderly manner. The positive feedback he received from his contribution to the meal gave him the positive attention that he craved, even without any of his clownish routines.

Harry's recipes demonstrated his affection for good food, travel, and good times. In the kitchen, he performed in an age-appropriate fashion when reminded that he was a young adult and expected to perform at that level.

HAPPY HARRY'S SOUTHWESTERN MEATLOAF
Serves 8 (or 4 very hungry people)

INGREDIENTS
1 small green pepper
2 lbs ground beef (can substitute ground turkey)
1 envelope dried onion soup mix (Lipton's Secrets is recommended)
2 cups crushed cornflake crumbs or dried bread crumbs
1½ cups thawed frozen, steamed, or drained canned whole kernel yellow corn

¾ cup water
1/3 cup ketchup
2 eggs, beaten
Salsa, grated cheese, optional

DIRECTIONS
Preheat oven to 350 degrees
Grease 13" x 9" baking pan or spray well with cooking oil
Wash green pepper, remove seeds and core, and chop into bite-sized pieces
In large bowl, combine all ingredients, (except salsa and grated cheese). Mix together well and place in greased baking pan.
Bake one hour, or until meat is no longer pink and is firm to touch.
Drain meatloaf if any grease has been released.
Let stand for 10 minutes before slicing.
Serve sliced with salsa and grated cheese, if desired.

Greg's personal characteristics were put to great use in the kitchen. He was an enigma. Although in some other classes, he displayed a negative, aggressive influence; in this class he often demonstrated a gentle, patient style that might have been overlooked. When following a recipe, preparing food, setting the table, or cleaning up after a meal, he provided a valuable influence. The kind nature displayed some weeks allowed him to help other students who were not as confident of their cooking skills as he was. He was a role model and a helpful assistant in many sessions. His serious and thoughtful nature made his contributions to the discussions unique. Although there were some weeks when he reverted back to the style he displayed in most other areas, he was usually positive in this class. Perhaps it was his feelings of competence or his need for order and structure that made the pieces come together in this setting, or maybe he enjoyed eating and liked to taste the product of his labors.

Becca presented a different challenge. Although she had some experience, skill, and interest in cooking, her inability to focus on anything but her own needs at the moment, made it difficult for her to follow through with class expectations. She sought attention in negative ways, which concerned both the teacher and the other students. She enjoyed eating, and could with direct attention read a recipe, perform all the required skills to follow the recipe, measure ingredients, prepare the food, set the table, and clean up after the meal. However, most weeks, she spent most of her time complaining or seeking attention for some issue not directly connected to the tasks on which we were focusing. It led to frustration in the class and did not help move her forward in her goals to achieve independence. It will be important for Becca to learn and remember this message from an anonymous source: "Remember, people will judge you by your actions, not your intentions. You may have a heart of gold—but so does a hard-boiled egg." Although the potential was there, she was not yet able to resist her inclination to drop back to a mode of interaction more typical of a much younger, less capable child, rather than the functional young adult that she could be. So that she can be given the respect that she craves, it will be essential that Becca find the resources, with assistance and attention, to demonstrate her potential on a more consistent basis. She cannot only make vague promises, but she will need to come through and perform.

Promising to prepare shepherd's pie, finally delivering the recipe after persuasion, and then "spraining" her ankle the day that she was to be the head chef, didn't work that day, nor will it in the long range future. The big question is how to convince her that she must take the responsibility for the change.

Will didn't feel confident in many areas of his life. Although he had a strong interest in history and athletics, he was not always willing or able to use his interests to allow him to try new experiences. He did use his knowledge and affection for sports to find a seasonal dream job with a local sports team. When he felt unsure of himself, he usually displayed a negative attitude that closed off his opportunities to consider and learn new options. His appreciation of good food allowed him to share some of his favorite recipes and to enjoy his role as head chef when he offered these recipes. In the kitchen, when Will assumed the role as the class leader for the day, he was able to display his finest characteristics, his energy and his ability to take charge and give suggestions to the other students. However, when he was not in that position, he often became de-energized and required a great deal of encouragement to start moving. This characteristic was not that unusual with this population of students for whom learning was so challenging. Will needed to find a way to take best advantage of his comfort zone on a consistent basis, which would help build confidence and break the negatively reinforcing cycle. Hopefully, continued success and positive reinforcement will help him break free.

Will had a well-developed sense of pride. He was strong-willed and wanted to do things his way. He was sure that he had the answers and worked hard to prove to others that he was right. When it came to cooking, he usually was right. He enjoyed cooking healthy, tasty selections and set good examples for his classmates on how to accomplish the tasks necessary to make the meal. When he was able to demonstrate his competence it made it easier for others to follow his example. This lasagna is a good example of a nutritious, delicious meal that can be prepared ahead of time, refrigerated, and reheated. It can even be frozen and served at another time.

VEGETARIAN LASAGNA
Serves 8-10

INGREDIENTS
1 8-oz package frozen spinach OR 16 oz fresh, pre-washed spinach

3 garlic cloves

1 zucchini

8 oz sliced mushrooms

1 green or red bell pepper

Olive oil for sautéing

1 lb ricotta cheese (regular, skim milk, or non-fat)

½ cup grated parmesan cheese

2 eggs, beaten

2 tbs fresh basil, oregano, or thyme or 2 tsp dried Italian seasoning

32 oz tomato sauce (can be combination of 26 oz prepared sauce and 1 8-oz can tomato paste)

One package no-boil lasagna noodles

8 oz mozzarella cheese

Salt/pepper

DIRECTIONS
Grease 13"x9" baking pan.

Preheat oven to 375 degrees.

Thaw frozen spinach (if using fresh just proceed with recipe).

Peel and mince garlic. Slice zucchini and mushrooms. Wash, seed, and slice or dice pepper. (Use only the vegetables and quantities you prefer.)

Sauté minced garlic in bit of oil for few minutes to soften.

Combine ricotta cheese, parmesan cheese, and eggs. Add spinach to this mixture.

Add seasoning mixture and garlic to tomato sauce. Spread one cup of tomato sauce on bottom of prepared pan.

Arrange one layer of uncooked noodles on top of sauce.

Add layer of ricotta mixture. Sprinkle with mozzarella cheese.

Start next layer with noodles, then sauce, then cheese, etc.

End layering with tomato sauce and mozzarella cheese, setting aside a small amount of parmesan and mozzarella for topping.

Cover with aluminum foil and bake for 30-35 minutes. Remove foil, spread with last sprinkle of parmesan cheese and mozzarella. Return to oven for 5-10 minutes until bubbly. Remove from oven and let sit for 5 minutes before serving.

Francesca had many secret abilities. She tended to be a tease and rarely demonstrated her capacity until put to a test. Her cooking comfort was revealed early in the semester. Although she liked to hide it, she was often a "go-to-girl" when students had questions about how to handle any challenging assignments in the cooking process. This recipe was tasty, easy and nutritious. It could become a perfect meal with the addition of a few vegetables. Adding spinach, mushrooms, or sautéed peppers would provide samples from all of the daily recommended food categories.

BBQ CHICKEN PIZZA
Serves 4-6

INGREDIENTS
2 tbs olive oil
½ lb chicken tenders (thinly sliced boneless chicken breasts)
2/3 cup prepared barbecue sauce (Bull's-Eye Original recommended)
Flour for dusting surface
1 13-oz package pizza dough (Pillsbury Classic recommended)
¾ cup shredded Gouda cheese
1 cup shredded mozzarella cheese
¾ shredded parmesan cheese
½ medium red onion, peeled and thinly sliced
3 tbs chopped fresh cilantro leaves (optional)

DIRECTIONS
Preheat oven to 400 degrees.
Heat oil in large skillet over medium-high heat. Add chicken tenders and sauté until golden brown, about 12 minutes. Remove from heat. When chicken is cool enough to handle, dice into small pieces (should be a bit more than 1 cup of meat). Toss chicken with 3 tbs barbecue sauce. Set aside.
On floured surface, roll out pizza dough and place on greased pan (pizza pan or cookie sheets). Spread out into 15x10-inch rectangle or 14-inch circle. Spread remaining barbecue sauce over dough. Sprinkle

with onion and cheeses. (Other vegetables can be added; spread them around before adding cheese.)

Bake for 20 minutes until crust is browned and cheese is melted and bubbly.

For some students, other than their relationships with peers, which certainly was important, little in the college experience excited them. They were not troublesome, but they couldn't seem to find a niche where they could become involved. They did satisfactory work in class but seemed to be searching for the thing that would be the "turn-on" key. Max was a bit of a Renaissance man, enjoying travel and exotic food. Helping him find his niche was the challenge.

Max tended to be quiet and rather disengaged in most classes. He really liked to cook and eat so he was more engaged and enthusiastic in Food Lab. He traveled extensively with his family and sampled foods from around the world. His recipes selections were representative of his travels and tastes. Although the recipes that he selected were unfamiliar to many of the students, they enjoyed the flavors and the stories of the trips where Max had tasted the foods.

APRICOT COUSCOUS
Serves 4-6 as a side dish

INGREDIENTS
Extra virgin olive oil
1 small red onion, diced into small pieces
¼ cup dried apricots, coarsely chopped
¼ cup whole almonds, toasted and coarsely chopped
1 cup couscous
1½ cups chicken stock, warmed
½ tsp lemon zest
2 scallions, green parts only, sliced into thin rings
¼ cup fresh mint leaves, roughly chopped
½ bunch fresh cilantro leaves, roughly chopped
Kosher salt and freshly ground pepper

DIRECTIONS
Preheat oven to 350 degrees. When warm, toast almonds on cookie sheet. Shake pan occasionally while toasting 5-8 minutes until lightly browned. Remove from oven.

In medium saucepan over low heat, combine 2 tbs olive oil, chopped red onion, chopped apricot, and toasted almonds. Cook and stir until ingredients are soft and begin to smell good.

Add couscous, then stir in chicken broth. Add lemon zest and cover. Remove from heat.

Uncover pot, add scallions, mint, and cilantro. Fluff with fork.

Season with salt and pepper and toss gently to combine.

It was sometimes difficult to understand how and why Megan made decisions. She was an attractive, competent young lady who seemed able to do whatever she set out to do. She did well in most of her classes; she made strides in becoming a capable child care provider; she made and kept friends, but for some reason she did not feel confident. It was when she was head chef assuming leadership in Food Lab that the real Megan shone through. Perhaps one of the issues that held her back was some homesickness. Cooking reminded her of her family and might have comforted her and given her some assurance.

Although Megan was one of those people who could do most things well, she did not always sense the competence that she demonstrated and therefore needed reassurance to help her get over some gaps in her self-confidence. She was very proud of this recipe. Once people tasted the warm, rich delicious combination of flavors, it became one of their favorites, also. The praise that she received as she prepared and served her selections, helped to boost her self-assurance and acceptance.

HOMEMADE HASH BROWN POTATOES AND EGGS DELIGHT
Serves 4-6

INGREDIENTS
4 large potatoes
3 tbs butter
1 tbs minced onion (or dried onion flakes)
1 tsp salt
¼ tsp pepper
¼ cup milk
2 eggs
3 oz shredded cheese

DIRECTIONS
Scrub potatoes. You can peel them or leave them unpeeled. Slice potatoes, then chop into bite-sized pieces. Place in microwave-safe pot with small pat of butter and cook at high heat for 8 minutes. Check to see that the potatoes are tender but not mushy (remember to open cooking pan away from face and use hot pads). Let cool to room temperature. Potatoes can be boiled on stove also; boil for 10-12 minutes then check texture.

Melt butter in large skillet over medium heat. Combine potatoes, onions, salt and pepper. (You can add milk to this mixture, or can reserve milk to scramble with eggs.) When butter is melted and hot, add potato mixture. Press down firmly. Reduce heat and fry slowly until bottom is golden brown. Do not stir while cooking. Turn potato mix over carefully and continue frying or can put under broiler to brown other side.

Once potatoes are ready, scramble eggs with 1-2 tbs milk or water. Pour into hot skillet and mix until set to your taste.

Pour eggs over potatoes; melt shredded cheddar cheese over eggs and potatoes. Serve warm.

Because David was shy, he did not tend to communicate verbally with ease, but he was able to share information by demonstrating how to do something. He traveled widely with his family and enjoyed sharing his knowledge of food from other countries. Once we were enjoying his selections, he was much more comfortable speaking about his experiences.

SPICED PEANUT FLAVORED SESAME NOODLES
Serves 4

INGREDIENTS
4-5 cloves of garlic
6-7 scallions, or green onions, peeled
½ cup creamy peanut butter
2 tbs rice vinegar
½ tsp ground ginger
2 tbs low sodium soy sauce
4 tbs sugar
2 tbs dark sesame oil
½ tsp crushed red pepper (for milder sauce, use less red pepper, or for even spicier, add more)
1 lb package spaghetti, cooked and drained

DIRECTIONS:
Chop scallions and garlic finely in a food processor, using on/off turns. Add remaining sauce ingredients (everything but the pasta) and process until smooth.

(Or, if preparing by hand, mince scallions and garlic until fine. Combine liquid ingredients and spices and then mix in peanut butter.)

Prepare pasta according to package directions. Drain and rinse.

Toss sauce over hot pasta and serve immediately.

Here is another example of Max's travel experiences. Good conversation usually developed when a student shared a recipe typical of an international cuisine. Students discussed their foreign travel experiences and their comfort levels with foods and spices from different places and cultures.

PAD THAI (WITH CHICKEN)
Serves 4-6

INGREDIENTS:
1 12-oz package of rice noodles
2 tbs butter
1 lb boneless, skinless chicken cut into bite-sized pieces (shrimp can be substituted)
¼ cup vegetable oil
3 eggs
1 tbs white wine vinegar
2 tbs Thai fish sauce
3 tbs white sugar
1/8 tsp crushed, dried red pepper flakes
2 cups bean sprouts
4 cups crushed roasted peanuts
3 green onions, peeled and sliced into thin rings
(May be served with cooked white rice, optional)

DIRECTIONS:
Soak rice noodles by covering with cold water in large pot for 30-50 minutes or until soft. Drain and set aside.

Heat butter in wok or large skillet. Sauté chicken pieces until lightly browned. Remove from pan and set aside. Heat ¼ cup oil in wok or skillet over medium heat. Crack eggs into hot oil, stirring until firm. Stir in chicken and cook for 5 minutes. Add softened noodles, vinegar, fish sauce, sugar, and red pepper flakes. Taste to adjust seasoning. Mix while cooking to soften noodles. Add bean sprouts and cook together for 3-5 more minutes.

Serve with peanuts, green onions, and cooked white rice.

This recipe, adapted from the cooking magazine Bon Appetit, *was a more complicated version of standard chicken parmesan. Ben took his cooking seriously and wanted to share one of his favorites. He was a quiet, thoughtful student who needed to gain confidence in his abilities. His pride and comfort cooking provided a baseline from which he could grow. From this recipe, students learned how to make a red sauce from scratch.*

SOPHISTICATED CHICKEN PARMESAN
Serves 8-10

INGREDIENTS
<u>Basic Tomato Sauce</u>
¼ cup extra-virgin olive oil
1¾ cups chopped onions
4 garlic cloves, minced
¾ cup peeled and coarsely grated carrots
3 tbs chopped fresh thyme or 1 tsp dried thyme flakes
2 28-oz cans whole tomatoes in juice
Salt, pepper, Italian seasoning to taste

<u>Chicken</u>
2 boneless, skinless chicken breast halves
3 cups bread crumbs
2 large eggs
1 cup flour
8 tbs or more olive oil, as needed
3 cups mozzarella cheese
1¼ cups parmesan cheese (divided)
1¼ cups Pecorino Romano cheese (divided)
2 tbs chopped fresh parsley
1 tbs fresh marjoram, chopped (optional)

DIRECTIONS
Heat olive oil in large saucepan over medium-high heat Add onions and garlic; sauté until onions are soft and golden, about 10 minutes. Add carrots and thyme; sauté until carrots are soft, about 5 minutes. Add tomatoes with juice; bring to boil while crushing the tomatoes with a

potato masher or a big fork. Reduce heat to medium-low; simmer until sauce thickens and is reduced (about 20 minutes). Season to taste with salt and pepper and Italian spices. Cool slightly. Cover and refrigerate. (Sauce can be made 1 day ahead. Rewarm before using.)

Place chicken breast halves between 2 sheets of plastic wrap. Using meat mallet or rolling pin, pound chicken to 1/3 inch thickness. Sprinkle both sides of chicken with salt and pepper. Spread bread crumbs on plate. Whisk eggs in bowl. Spread flour in another bowl. Dip chicken into flour, then egg, then bread crumbs until well coated.

Preheat oven to 350 degrees. Heat 2 tbs oil in large nonstick skillet over medium high heat. Brown chicken in batches, adding oil as needed. Drain chicken when browned.

Grease 15"x10"x2" baking pan. Spread 1 cup tomato sauce over bottom of pan. Arrange layer of chicken over sauce. Sprinkle mozzarella cheese, then parmesan and Romano. Cover with another layer of tomato sauce, chicken, cheeses. Bake until cheeses melt and chicken is cooked through, about 20 minutes.

Sprinkle with parsley to serve.

CHAPTER 11

CHILDHOOD OBESITY

In 2010, thanks to the attention being given in part by the First Lady, Michelle Obama, a new awareness and consideration is being devoted to a developing health crisis. Jamie Oliver, a British chef and personality, hosted a primetime TV program trying to make an impact on the national conscience. Even with all this heightened consciousness, the fact remains that young children are gaining weight out of proportion to their age and height. This concern continues for both individuals and society. There are so many factors to consider that are not directly related to the goals of this piece of work, but I do feel some responsibility to discuss and examine a few issues that do directly relate. We know that each person brings his/her own eating history to this class. Laurie Colwin said, "No one who cooks, cooks alone. Even at her most solitary, a cook in the kitchen is surrounded by generations of cooks past, the advice and menus of cooks present, the wisdom of cookbook writers."

And so each student brought a bit of his/her own heritage to the class. We learned that some families tended to dine in restaurants or bring in prepared foods, while others came with a broad cooking tradition and more often cooked from recipes or history at home. However or wherever they got their sustenance, they tended to follow the eating habits they were taught, by example if nothing else, in their homes. Most people remember the first time they were placed in a strange place alone for an extended period of time having to eat in a new environment. For some people, it might have been summer camp, a visit with a relative, or first year at a boarding school or residential college. Suddenly, you were on your own to make food choices. Usually the food was dramatically different than what you were accustomed to at home and no one was watching what you selected. I don't know about your first example of this experience was but for me, it was my freshman year at college. The traditions of the all female college of a bigger university that I attended required the first-year "girls" to have dinner together every night during the week and Sunday brunch in the dining hall. We could control exactly what or how much we ate, but since we were required to show up at those meals, essentially the dining service made our broad choices for us.

The "mystery meats" and strange combinations of foods were sometimes alarming. It was challenging to figure out how to maintain some semblance of nutrition and taste given some of the food options that were available to us. Many students sat at the table, socialized with their peers, made plans for the weekend, and went back to the dorms and ordered out. The rush to classes in the morning often meant grabbing a quick coffee and donut for breakfast. So, the famous "freshman fifteen," describing the number of pounds gained or lost during the first year, was not surprising. The first exposure to food freedom, without any familiar options, led to confusion and wonder. For some, it meant eating more junk food, less basics. For others, it meant eating more or less quantity, resulting in dramatic weight fluctuations. It was very rare, if not impossible, for a student to manage to find and eat a perfectly balanced, nutritious, tasty meal to match his/her own particular needs and tastes in those days. Even now, when students have the chance to have mini refrigerators in their room, it is rare to find many students who stock yogurt, fresh fruit, and fruit juice in their refrigerators. Even when dining services are much more attuned to health requirements and personal preferences and offer a much broader range of options, it is a challenge for some students to learn to manage their daily diet.

Much of the research on childhood obesity has indicated that lack of education and exercise on the part of both the child and the parents frequently lead to the problems of weight management. We have learned that there are many potential negative health consequences of being overweight. When children are living at home and their parents/relatives do not know how or what can provide the essential elements of healthy eating, or do not have the time or the income to produce healthy meals, it is difficult for the children to establish better eating patterns. In 2010, Jamie Oliver hosted a program trying to educate a whole community in West Virginia to improve their eating habits. He had a tough time in the beginning convincing influential people that it was worth their while to control the fat and sugar in local children's diets. He stressed eating locally produced, nutritious, fresh food rather than sweetened, packaged food. His program took time and money to convince the school system to make changes in the food they served the young children. They all learned the realities of eating healthy. It remains to be seen if there will be long-lasting benefits for the whole community. Hopefully for the few families that he touched personally there will be dramatic changes in their eating habits. Perhaps they will be able to set examples for their friends and neighbors.

There are some grants available to help young people create and implement local, hands-on programs to fight childhood obesity. Each grant also engages participating youth in service learning, an effective teaching and learning strategy that supports student learning, academic achievement, and workplace readiness. In reports received by United Health Group and Youth Service America, more than 99 percent of the organizations that participated in the program agreed that the projects improved the students' knowledge and awareness of childhood obesity and led them to adopt healthier eating habits.

Peggy Orenstein said in the *New York Times Magazine* on April 18, 2010, "Food is never just food. Food is love. Food is solace, it is politics. It is religion." She suggested that what a parent feeds a child could become a measure of their parenting skills. It seems, in certain communities, what the children eat for lunch reflects on the parent's worth and sense of commitment to the child. So as I meet all the Threshold students, I am often surprised to note that even for students who come from homes with well-educated parents, awareness of basic healthy eating habits is not uniformly established. Many students contribute recipes that they have come to know and enjoy. Some of the students come from homes where they have been taught by example ways that people can eat a variety of tasty and healthy meals. Billy, the son of a doctor, contributed a recipe for whole-wheat pasta with sautéed vegetables. He really liked mushrooms and asparagus, but since some of his classmates found these particular vegetables distasteful, we discussed all the many options of fresh vegetables that could be sliced and stir-fried with olive oil to put over the pasta. Everyone enjoyed this meal and perhaps a few of the students learned alternative ways to satisfy their hunger without sacrificing their health.

Throughout the year, we discussed how the students could learn to prepare a tasty, healthy menu within their own time and money guidelines. There are so many other options that can meet these criteria once a pattern is established. However, for some other students, the eating habits that they have learned are not as well balanced or thoughtful. For this group, it is much more challenging to break the patterns and think about how to watch their nutrition and their budget, while preparing simple foods that they like to eat. Most people need to be taught at some time to accomplish their health care goals. They also have to learn to value their own health and well-being and to recognize that they can have some impact by eating well and getting enough sleep.

CHAPTER 12

CONCLUSION

I know that we cannot go into people's homes or instruct every family how to eat, but it seems to me that as a society we need to educate children, from an early age, what food choices they have and the long range consequences of their decisions. A class similar to Food Lab could be offered to provide that wide range of education, socialization, personal development and social awareness. We could start our own food revolution that could have a lasting impact on the next generation.

Every young adult needs to establish healthy eating habits. For those dealing with learning issues and other special needs, it is even more essential. Dealing with all the challenges of independent living is an enormous undertaking. For recent graduates or for others starting to live on their own, developing basic routines that offer good nutrition and thoughtful general health habits is important just so they do not undermine their own well-being. This can also help offer a foundation to supply the energy, concentration and attractive appearance that are necessary to take the required steps to support their independence. Eating a healthy meal is an essential first step in getting to an interview on time, appearing energetic, enthusiastic, and well-groomed. Having the knowledge and the right food available in the refrigerator is usually a better way to start each day than racing to the local coffee shop or fast food restaurant.

It has been a dream of mine to return to the old tradition of teaching home economics/cooking to every student. I believe that if a cooking course could be offered in middle school like in the "old days", just as adolescents begin to become more cognizant of their appearance and health, better habits could be established which could impact on their long range well-being.

Julia Child, cook and cookbook author (1912-2004) said it all when she said that people didn't have to cook fancy or complicated masterpieces, just good food from fresh ingredients. I hope people can use the material I have shared as just the beginning of the search for good nutrition and healthy eating habits. My dream also includes the idea that everyone can enjoy the delicious odors when the door is opened to a kitchen where a tasty meal is being produced. The other element offered by this dream include the sense of pride and satisfaction that one gains by sharing a meal with family and friends, eating together while developing relationships and social awareness.

Food has an awful lot to do with it. I wish each of you the opportunity to discover more of your identity through cooking and tasting your own homemade meals. I hope that more educators can take advantage of this wonderful opportunity to become familiar with their students in this unique way, while offering the young people the chance to gain skills and potential for better health. Cook well. Eat well. Enjoy!

REFERENCES:

Brooks, R. (2001) *Raising Resilient Children*, Chicago, Contemporary Books

Brooks,R. (newsletters@drrobertbrooks.com)

Colwin, Laurie (1993) *A Writer Returns to the Kitchen,* New York, New York: Harper Collins

Gladwell, Malcolm (2000) *The Tipping Point:* Little, Brown and Company

Greenspan, Stanley, Ira, M.D. (2010) Obituary, *Boston Globe,* Friday, April 30, p B13

Grossman, H. (1983) *Classification in Mental Retardation.* Washington, DC American Association on Mental Deficiency.

Halpern, A. (1985). "Transition: A Look at the Foundations." *Exceptional Children 51,* 479-486.

Maslow, A (1943) *A Theory of Human Motivation,* originally published in *Psychological Review,* vol.50 #4, pp.370-396.

Narins, R. (2009) From *Michael Pollan's Food Quotes.*

nytimes.com/interactive/2009/10/11/magazine.20091011-foodrules. htmlpg2

Orenstein, P. (2010) "The Fat Trap." *New York Times Magazine,* April 18, 2010, p15.

Osten, F. (2009). "Where Life Has Taken Them: A Longitudinal Outcome Study of Threshold Graduates." Unpublished report.

Reiss, S. (2000) *Who Am I? The 16 Basic Desires that Motivate Our Behavior and Define Our Personalities,* New York: Tarcher/Putnam, pp17-18.

Roffman, A, Osten, F., Noveck, C (2009) Lesley University Centennial Publication

Seligman, Martin. (1991) *Helplessness:On Development, Depression and Death*, New York: W.H Freeman

Sitlington, P. & F.A. (1990) "Are Adolescents with Learning Disabilities Successfully Crossing the Bridge into Adult Life?" *Learnng Disabilities Quarterly,* 13, 97.

University of Southern Australia (2002) Study of motivation with template prepared by Flexible Learning Center

Will, M. (1984) OSERS Programming for the Transition of Youth with Disabilities: Bridges from School to Working Life. Washington, DC: Office of Special Education and Rehabilitation Services.

Wizenberg, M. (2009) *A Homemade Life.* New York, New York: Simon & Schuster, p2

Wills, Monica (2009) *Cowboy & Will: A Love Story.* New York, New York: Simon & Schuster, p39

RECIPE INDEX

Breakfast/Brunch/ Egg Dishes:
    Chocolate Chip Pancakes (20)
    Cornmeal Jonny Cakes and Fried Plantains (55)
    Grandma's Sicilian Tomatoes and Eggs (117)
    Fancy Stuffed French Toast (45)
    Homemade Hash Browns and Eggs (132)
    Nutritious and Delicious Egg Beaters Omelet (42)
    Quickie Quiche (119)

Appetizers:
    Arielle's Super Samosas (53)
    Artichoke Dip (112)

Salad
    Incredible Chopped Salad (99)

Soups:
    Creamy Clam Chowder (96)
    French Onion Soup (113)
    Russian Summer Soup (64)
    Southwestern Vegetable Soup (27)

Pasta/Rice/Pizza
    Any Time Noodles and Rice (100)
    Armenian Rice Pilaf (62)
    Deep Dish Pizza (24)

French Bread Pizza (115)
Gluten free, Lactose free and Delicious Lasagna (93)
Golden Baked Macaroni and Cheese (110)
Linguini and Shrimp Scampi (79)
Luscious Linguini (101)
Pad Thai (135)
Pasta with Clam Sauce (73)
Spiced Peanut Noodles (134)
Tasty Sesame Noodles (85)

Vegetarian Entrees
Apricot Couscous (129)
Potato pancakes/ Applesauce (87/89)
Remarkable Eggplant Parmesan (83)
Vegetarian Lasagna (126)

Chicken Entrees
BarBQ Chicken Pizza (128)
Chicken Paprikash (75)
Chicken Marsala (77)
General Gao's Chicken (49)
Sophisticated Chicken Parmesan (136)
Paella Express (20)

Beef Entrees
Danielle's Homemade Marinara and Meatballs (36)
Hago's Tips-Beef Kifto (65)
Harry's Southwest Meatloaf (123)
Peruvian Lomo Saltado (58)
Sloppie Joe's with a Secret (107)

Desserts and Sweets:
Chocolate Kiss Cookies (16)
Happy Holiday Delights (28)
Lithuanian Apple Crumb Cake (60)
Peanut Butter Delight (29)
Old Favorite Rice Krispie Treats (26)
Whole Egg Sponge Cake (91)